Bennet with Jung at Bollingen

Bennet with Jung at Küsnacht

Bennet with Jung at lakeside at Bollingen

C. G. JUNG

E. A. BENNET

CHIRON PUBLICATIONS
Asheville, North Carolina

First published 1961 by E. A. Bennet.
Barrie & Rockliff (Barrie Books Ltd.)
2 Clement's Inn London WC2
Printed in Great Britain at
The University Press
Aberdeen

Cover photo of C.G. Jung reproduced by permission of Ruth Bailey.
Interior photos of C.G. Jung and E.A. Bennet reproduced by permission of the Bennet estate.

Library of Congress Cataloging-in-Publication Data

Bennet, E. A. (Edward Armstrong)
C. G. Jung / E. A. Bennet.
p. cm.—(Polarities of the psyche)
Originally published: London : Barrie & Rockliff, 1961.
Includes bibliographical references and index.
ISBN 978-1-63051-537-9 (alk. paper)
1. Jung, C. G. (Carl Gustav), 1875–1961. I. Title: Carl Gustav Jung. II. Title. III. Series.
BF109.J8B4 2006
150.19'54092—dc22

2005034044

CONTENTS

PREFACE

For many readers of his books, C. G. Jung is but a name and Jung as a person is hardly discernible. To depict some of the 'key' aspects of Jung's work in the setting of his personality is the aim of the chapters which follow. Each section of the book might be looked on as an annotation, a supplementary note, rather than a summary of Jung's teaching, which is already available and is mentioned here in footnotes for the guidance of the reader. The selected subject-matter—and the reasons for the choice and for the decision to omit other topics—has been discussed with Jung from time to time when I have been his guest at Küsnacht on the Lake of Zürich or at his 'weekend' house near Bollingen, a quiet village on the shores of the same lake. An effort has been made to indicate the medical background of his work, and Jung, always mindful of his profession, approved of this and agreed that personal references to him might well be apposite.

A previous plan was that I should write his biography. We spent some time on this project, and he gave me a great deal of information about his childhood, his family, his career, and the development of his ideas. But on reflection he thought this would be an almost impossible undertaking because of the variety of his work and the complexity of his personality. In the end he decided that he must write an autobiography, and he has done so (as part of a book written by C. G. Jung and Aniela Jaffé). He finished this far from congenial task—as he described it—in September 1959 and, as it happened, I was staying with him at the time.

It seemed probable that this book, although in a different setting, would overlap the autobiography in some ways, but Jung thought this unlikely and in any case unimportant.

Much of the material has been used in seminars at the Royal Bethlem and Maudsley Hospital and in post-graduate lectures at the Institute of Psychiatry, Maudsley Hospital, London University. Students often were kind enough to suggest publication of the lectures, and this has been done here to a limited extent. But there have been many additions for the information of those who are interested in Jung as a man—a subject about which there is considerable curiosity and speculation, if one might judge from the questions asked about his personality and way of life.

E. A. Bennet
London, 30th May, 1961

Professor Jung died on 6th June 1961, a few days after this book had gone to press. In January of this year while I was staying with him at Küsnacht-Zürich, he was kind enough to read the whole of the book, then in typescript. He made many suggestions and corrections in his own handwriting. It may be assumed, therefore, that the statements made here are in accordance with his views.

E. A. B.
6th June, 1961

FOREWORD

'WHAT book on Jung should I read?' is a question that is often posed by people who are new to the subject. Whilst there has been a steady stream of introductory books and biographical studies on Jung, the work which I have invariably recommended is the present one, which, after more than forty years, is now finally back in print.

Before considering this work, a word or two concerning its author is order.[1] Edward Armstrong Bennet was born in the village of Poyntzpass in County Armagh, Northern Ireland, on 21 October 1888. He was the youngest of five children, an identical twin. His father was fifty-six when he was born and died of kidney failure eight years later. Six months after that, his eldest brother died of tuberculosis, aged fifteen. Thus a happy rural life came to a sudden end. The twins were dispatched to an uncle in the south of Ireland and the remnants of the family moved to Belfast.

Bennet later rejoined the family and went on to study philosophy, theology and classics at Trinity College, Dublin, graduating in 1910. He attended theological college in Cambridge and was ordained as an Anglican priest in 1913. The following year the First World War broke out and he straightaway joined the army as a chaplain to the 6th Northamptonshire Regiment. He was awarded the Military Cross in 1916 for 'conspicuous gallantry and devotion to duty', and in 1917, after two and a half years of

1. I would like to thank Eveline Bennet and Glin Bennet for biographical information.

the horrors of the trenches in France, he was posted to Mesopotamia (now Iraq). It was during this time that he planned to study medicine, with a view to practising psychiatry. He took his medical degrees back again at Trinity College, and conducted church services to help with the fees.

After qualifying in 1925, he moved to London to work under Hugh Crichton-Miller[2] at Bowden House Nursing Home; he took up appointments also at the new Institute of Medical Psychology (now the Tavistock Clinic) and at the West End Hospital for Nervous Diseases. As soon as the Second World War broke out he was back in the army, and latterly, with the rank of brigadier, he was head of psychiatric services for what would now be the Indian sub-continent.

His correspondence with Jung dates from 1933, and they met in 1935 when Jung delivered his lectures on 'Fundamental Psychological Conceptions' to the Institute of Medical Psychology in London (known as 'the Tavistock Lectures').[3] Michael Fordham recalled that Bennet was 'the only man I know to become a close friend of Jung, though a number of people have claimed that distinction!'[4] Fordham also noted that 'It was a friendship that was, no doubt, fertilised by their mutual interest in both psychology and religion.'[5]

After the Second World War, Bennet was appointed a consultant psychotherapist to the Maudsley Hospital and as a lecturer at the Institute of Psychiatry. In this post-graduate context, he lectured on analytical psychology, which led to an influx of psychiatrically trained candidates to the newly established Society of Analytical Psychology. Bennet joined the Society but became critical of the

2. Crichton-Miller was a friend of Jung. See Jung's tribute to him in *Collected Works* 18, 1462–1465.
3. Bennet wrote a foreword to the paperback edition of these lectures, *Analytical Psychology: Its Theory and Practice* (London, Routledge and Kegan Paul, 1968).
4. Michael Fordham, *The Making of an Analyst: A Memoir* (London, Free Associations, 1993).
5. Michael Fordham, obituary of Bennet, *The Lancet*, 2 April 1977, p. 763.

direction which it took, and eventually resigned. His standing in the psychiatric world did much to raise the profile of analytical psychology in Great Britain. In 1952, he wrote an unsigned leader on Jung for the *British Medical Journal*, entitled, 'A Great Thinker'.[6] In 1952, his first wife, Flora Newbery (née Wylie), with whom he had two sons, died. He retired from the Maudsley in 1955. In 1958, he married Eveline Routh. He published a number of articles and reviews on psychological and therapeutic topics. The present book was his first one, and was published in 1961, shortly after Jung's death. He followed this in 1966 with another introductory work on Jung, *What Jung Really Said*, which presented a fuller account of Jung's theories.[7] In 1971, he was a Founding Fellow of the Royal College of Psychiatrists, and a Fellow of the British Psychological Society. He died in 1977. It was noted that he was unusual among psychiatrists in that while his predominant interest and practice were in analytical psychotherapy he did not exclude the use of physical methods of treatment or indeed any measure that he thought likely to help his patients. Indeed, he was distinguished throughout his life by independence of judgement and lack of prejudice; he did not believe that Jungian analysis was the only valid form of approach to human problems, and often referred to Jung's own reluctance to form a school based on his teachings.[8]

It is worth tracing the genesis of Bennet's book, as it helps to explain what is unique about it. In the 1950s, there were several attempts to write biographies of Jung, the most famous being Aniela Jaffé's project, which resulted in *Memories, Dreams, Reflections*.[9]

6. *British Medical Journal*, 9 February 1952, pp. 314–6.
7. (London, Macdonald).
8. Obituary of Bennet, *British Medical Journal*, 19 March 1977, vol. 1. On 20 January 1939, Jung wrote a letter in appreciation of Bennet's article 'Individualism in Psychotherapy' (*British Journal of Medical Psychology* 16, 1938, pp. 298–306), describing it as 'a very valuable criticism of that ridiculous "Methodism" in psychotherapy.' Jung archives, Swiss Federal Institute of Technology, Zürich (hereafter, JA).
9. (London, Fontana, 1982).

After the Second World War, Bennet visited Jung on several occasions and stayed with him at his home in Küsnacht, as well at his retreat in Bollingen. Their conversations often covered historical topics, and Bennet became interested in writing a biography of Jung. On 5 September 1956, he wrote to Jung indicating that Ruth Bailey, Jung's friend who stayed with Jung to look after him after his wife died, had suggested that Bennet write a biography of Jung, and that H. L. Philp had suggested the same thing. On 10 October, Jung wrote to him:

> As you know, I am a somewhat complicated phenomenon, which hardly can be covered by one biographer only. . . . Therefore I should like to make you a similar proposition, namely that you proceed along your line as a medical man like Philp has done on his part as a theologian. Being a doctor you would inquire into the anamnesis of your patient and you would ask the questions and I would answer as a patient would answer. Thus you would move along the lines of your habitual thinking and would be enabled to produce a picture of my personality understandable at least to more or less medical people. Philp certainly would produce a picture of my religious aspect, equally satisfactory. Since it is undeniable that one of several aspects is medical, another theological, a biography written by specialists in their field has the best chance of being accurate, although not comprehensive in as much as the specifical psychological synthesis would demand somebody equally at home in primitive psychology, mythology, history, parapsychology and science—and even in the field of artistic experience.[10]

10. Jung archives, original in English. Howard Philp had also been considering a biographical work on Jung. After modifications, the outcome of Philp's project was his *Jung and the Problem of Evil* (1959). Jung's replies to his questions were also reproduced in *Collected Works* 18 under the title 'Jung and Religious Belief'.

Bennet accepted Jung's suggestion, and sent him a list of questions, mainly concerning his childhood.[11] Jung replied that it would take too long to give written answers, so he invited Bennet over for a fortnight.[12] He added the following reflections on the undertaking, which suggest that he preferred to convey his recollections in conversation, rather than to commit himself to writing:

> The whole thing is a ticklish task and it seems to be rather difficult because the average reader would hardly be capable of understanding what it is all about. I have been exposed to so many misunderstandings that I am rather scared to tell the truth about my biography, as I see it. I should therefore prefer, you should first try to find your way through the jungle of memories.[13]

Bennet went to stay with Jung between 3 and 12 January, and took notes of his conversations.[14] During these discussions, the project appears to have taken shape. On 14 January 1957, Bennet wrote to Jung, 'Your commendation of the plan that I should write a biography, based on your contributions to medicine, was most cheering.'[15] Regarding the potential overlap with Aniela Jaffé's project, Bennet added, 'There is no reason why this should clash with the plans of Frau Jaffé. So far as I could see she is concerned with your many interests and activities apart from the field of medicine.'[16]

Bennet then got to work on this project. The correspondence shows that he carefully checked with Jung concerning his recollections of what Jung had told him. He requested permission to use

11. Bennet to Jung, 7 December 1956, JA.
12. Jung to Bennet, 10 December 1956, JA, orig. in English.
13. *Ibid.*
14. *Meetings with Jung: Conversations Recorded by E. A. Bennet during the Years 1946–1961* (London, Anchor Press, 1982 / Zurich, Daimon Verlag, 1985). This volume contains critically important historical information.
15. JA.
16. *Ibid.*

some of the information which Jung had imparted to him. On 7 February 1959, Jung wrote to Bennet,

> Concerning your plan to write something about the 'development of my ideas and their impact on medicine', it pleases me very much. There are, of course, no objections from my part against your incorporating some of our early talks in the books.[17]

The work underwent a number of changes in the course of its composition. On 2 October 1959, Bennet wrote to Jung, 'The original form of the project which we discussed in writing a book about your work has of course undergone many modifications, and I am glad you think it is worthwhile going ahead in its present form.'[18]

On completing the work, Bennet submitted it to Jung. In January 1961, he went to stay with Jung and discussed the manuscript with him. On 17 January—the last time that they met—he noted, 'C. G. has finished reading my book; he told me it read easily and he thought highly of it, so that is satisfactory.'[19] After returning to London, Bennet wrote to Jung, 'It was extremely kind of you to spend so much time reading the typescript. All your suggestions are helpful and all will be incorporated.'[20]

Thus we see that Bennet's work arose out of a close collaboration with Jung, who had approved the final manuscript. Much of the biographical material had never before appeared in print. Thus in addition to serving its original purpose—providing a succinct overview of Jung's life and work—it forms an important primary source in its own right, not least because of the important correspondence with Jung on the question of science which he included.

17. JA, original in English.
18 JA.
19. *Meetings with Jung*, p. 124.
20. JA.

Bennet's book was eclipsed by *Memories, Dreams, Reflections*—not least because the latter was written in the first person and taken to be Jung's autobiography, as opposed to a biography, and had the benefit of the large publicity budget of a trade publisher.[21] Consequently, Bennet's book never received the attention it deserved.

Sonu Shamdasani
Reader in Jung History
Wellcome Trust Centre for the History of Medicine at University College London

21. Elsewhere, I have described how this became misperceived as Jung's 'autobiography' (*Jung Stripped Bare by His Biographers, Even,* London, Karnac, 2005), a source I have drawn upon here. See also Alan Elms, 'The Auntification of C. G. Jung,' in *Uncovering Lives: The Uneasy Alliance of Biography and Psychology* (New York, Oxford University Press, 1994). Bennet was almost alone in reviewers in not doing this. In his review in the *British Medical Journal*, he wrote, 'It is an unusual book and apparently it has been a great problem to reviewers, many of whom accepted it as an autobiography. Certainly it is not that' (23 September, 1963). Some of the biographical information from Jung in Bennet's book overlaps with the accounts in *Memories, Dreams, Reflections* (which Jung never approved the final manuscript of), but there are significant discrepancies. Bennet's versions also have the benefit of clearly differentiating his own comments and narration from what Jung told him.

CHAPTER ONE

Introduction to Jung

PROFESSOR C. G. JUNG, now eighty-five, has taken a leading part in altering the attitude of the physician and the layman towards sickness of the mind. When he was a student at Basel University, no one had heard of complexes, of introverts and extraverts, of mental conflict and dynamic psychology. Neither health nor sickness of mind was a subject of serious medical concern, and those in charge of lunatic asylums provided custodial care without thought of psychological treatment, mental structure, and psychopathology. Barbarities, taken for granted at one time, had passed: there were no fetters, and no society visitors gazed at the mentally deranged. By present standards, the nursing may not have been impressive, but physical violence was no longer used to drive out the evil spirits responsible for the disorder; there was a tolerant acceptance of the often amusing peculiarities of the insane, for whom no treatment was available beyond attention to bodily sickness. Here and there the mesmerists and hypnotists treated the symptoms of the less socially disturbed patients, often with considerable success, and left it at that. The mind itself remained a mystery. In the 'seventies and 'eighties Simon in France and Lombroso in Italy were keen observers of the bizarre pictures produced by the patients in mental asylums and attempted to understand them. But their reports had little effect upon treatment. An advance of importance came when the symptoms of mental illness had been classified and descriptive psychiatry encouraged at any rate a few doctors in charge of mental hospitals to think of insanity as a clinical problem.

Psychiatry was off the main road in medicine and had few attractions for the medical student. It was little wonder that Jung's friends and teachers thought him misguided when on qualification as a doctor he declined an offer as assistant to one of his teachers at Basel who had recently been appointed to a chair at a German university. In preference he took a position at the Burghölzli Hospital on the staff of Eugen Bleuler, Professor of Psychiatry in the University of Zürich. There he remained for eight years, and his work and that of his colleagues made the hospital famous. Freud and his small group, working in comparative obscurity in Vienna, were becoming known about the same time.

In those days no one would have guessed that we were at the beginning of a new era in psychiatry as well as in every other department of medicine. The mind itself had become a centre of interest and research, and this was destined to produce many unexpected results.

Jung's contribution to this changing scene has been continuous. His first publication came in 1902, and since then volume after volume has appeared. Some critics have hinted darkly that no one could have produced so much, that Jung got others to write his books, and that he added the finishing touches! His productivity is more easily explained: his education gave scope for his natural endowments and he learnt at an early age to think as he wrote, to say what he meant to say, to convey the impression he wished to convey. Sentence follows sentence rather slowly as he writes; but there are few alterations.

Like the other pioneers in psychiatry, Jung has had his share of criticism and misunderstanding. Even today observations about his work are produced with assurance by critics who know of it at second or even third hand. His books have the reputation of being difficult to understand, and there is a good deal of truth in this. We take it for granted that the physician or surgeon, concerned with the human body, must pursue his training over many years. Why should we expect that sound common sense is enough to grasp the mysterious workings of the mind? Of course Jung's books are difficult:

they cannot be read casually, for psychological understanding is not a natural endowment. The serious student, with sound training, will find Jung's books practical and informative. His breadth of scholarship may be rather alarming! But that is hardly a fault.

He describes himself as an empiricist—one who goes by experience—and this is accurate. Nevertheless, many think of him as a remote savant, propounding esoteric and mystical ideas. It is safe to say that the undefined mystical implies something obscure, of dark import, for the word is meant to convey a polite—or impolite!—rebuke when used by the critics of any psychological system with which they find themselves in disagreement. Dr. Ernest Jones tells us that 'Jung had revealed himself to me as a man with deep mystical tendencies'.[1] But Jung is not the only 'mystical' thinker. Freud's psychoanalysis was also considered by Hoche of Freiburg as 'an evil method born of mystical tendencies'.[2] And Dr. Edward Glover selects the same word when he declares that 'Orthodox Freudians have already challenged [the Klein theory] as a mystical deviation'.[3] A criticism of the Freudian theory in a well-known textbook on psychiatry strikes the same note: 'The criticisms to which Freudian theory can be subjected are so damaging, that it could hardly have lasted so long in its present form, were it not for the sectarian orthodoxy and the mystical halo by which it attracts its followers and adepts.'[4]

Mystical is about the last adjective his colleagues and acquaintances would use in describing Jung's active and stimulating personality; at all events, his 'deep mystical tendencies' are by no means obvious. For a visionary, he shows remarkable capacity for getting to the heart of practical problems in his work.

Jung writes with assurance, making his contribution modestly, without dogmatism, without claiming universal validity, for he

1. Jones, E., *Free Associations*, London, Hogarth Press (1959), p. 215.
2. Jones, E., *Sigmund Freud*, London, Hogarth Press (1955), Vol. II, p.131.
3. Glover, Edward, *Horizon* (1943), Vol. XI, No. 63, p. 211.
4. Mayer-Gross, W., Slater, Eliot, Roth, Martin, *Clinical Psychiatry*, London, Cassell (1954), p. 23.

knows how transitory, even futile, our hypotheses can be. A quality of charm and intimacy in style may lead the casual reader to conclude that the material is simple, obvious, and only common sense. Jung is under no such illusion; he has always been conscious of his own limitations in understanding the complexity of the mind. Though notable advances have been made in psychiatry, it is his opinion that the time is not ripe for pronouncements about psychology and psychiatry, for we have still much to learn. As a pioneer—as he himself has said—he has made all the mistakes pioneers are wont to make. Nevertheless, he has opened the way to a new understanding of the mind, healthy or sick. Nature has endowed him with an imaginative, original outlook, a balanced appreciation of facts—such as the facts of natural science—and, above all, the capacity to think. Systematic thinking is not so common as might be supposed, and inevitably it is associated with speculation and intuition. But however far his imagination may range, the facts, as he and others have observed them, are brought into focus before he advances a hypothesis or reaches a conclusion. Cautious withholding of judgment is characteristic of the Swiss people, perhaps because of their geographical situation. Jung is the typical Swiss thinker—alert, observant, critical, independent.

An author's personality is not always reflected in his writing, and this is true of Jung. Pupils who have talked to him and heard him lecture have a familiarity with his outlook which cannot be gained by reading his books. Consequently, those who know only his published works are at a disadvantage. Some readers seem to expect a finished system, consistent from beginning to end. They forget that Jung's thought has grown and expanded. It is easy to find petty discrepancies, and his critics will be certain to find what they are looking for. Once I asked Jung about some early views which appeared to conflict with later work. 'Of course there is a difference', he replied, 'that old stuff is cold soup.' There is nothing shallow in this. On the contrary, it must be so when there is development, growth, extension of thought. None of his hypotheses is sacrosanct to Jung; he is happy to abandon a point of view if another is shown to be more satisfactory, more in accordance with confirmed observation. It may happen that verification is difficult or seems impossible, and that, too, is important; it means that more work requires to be done. We would be foolish to give up what we know because there remains something not yet fully known.

In conversation and in lecturing he has the capacity to put new ideas very simply. Often his hearers feel the subject is already familiar. Perhaps they are right, and Jung would not disagree. On the other hand, he might well point out that their feeling of familiarity sprang from a subjective readiness to grasp a new concept of which, till then, they were unaware.

When conducting seminars he was courteous and attentive, and made his comments with complete naturalness; if anyone questioned his conclusions, his reply was definite and yet disarming: if the criticism was valid, he said so at once; if not, he gave his reasons. Nothing was left in doubt about his point of view. He was interested in comments following a lecture and delighted when a new idea was brought forward. On one occasion in a group discussion a questioner got into a protracted discussion with Jung, and this was boring to the others. Later someone remarked that his questioner had talked too much. "I don't agree at all,' said Jung. 'I was quite happy to let her talk, for then I could listen, which always suits me.' Jung was always interested to hear what a student had to say, and particularly so when the speaker stuck to his guns and really felt he had something to contribute. To have his own phrases and ideas handed back to him bored him. He welcomed those who challenged him, especially when they were evidently serious and not talking for the sake of talking. Many who have felt his power, his skill in making the abstruse seem simple, have copied his mannerisms, his turn of phrase, his gestures—even the type of pipe he smokes!

Jung's appearance is striking—tall, broad-shouldered, healthy-looking, with a cheerful, open face. Even today he could never be overlooked in any gathering. That his personality had a marked influence on an audience was obvious in his lecturing—and in his appearances on television. In 1935 he gave a course of five lectures in English at the Tavistock Clinic in London before a large and critical group of doctors. Listening to the lectures proved to be an unexpected experience to many, for from the start Jung held the audience as in a spell: there was complete silence and a feeling of anticipation. He was entirely at ease, totally free from shyness or stiffness in manner, and spoke for an hour or more out of his own experience, therefore with conviction—salted here and there with a nice sense of humour. Questions followed each lecture and the discussion had to be restricted to another hour.

During this visit to London, Jung had occasion to look up some references, and he went to the Reading Room of the British Museum. He was asked if he had a reader's ticket. 'No', he replied; 'I'm afraid I haven't. I did not know that was required.' 'Who are you?' he was asked. 'What is your name?' 'I am a Swiss doctor on a visit to London. My name is Jung—Dr. Jung.' 'Not, Freud, Jung, and Adler?' exclaimed the assistant. 'Oh, no,' he replied. 'Only Jung!'

Another instance of Jung's ability as a lecturer was evident in his Terry Lectures[5] at Yale University in 1937. Although he was accustomed to lecture in English, he asked that he might use the small hall, as he disliked crowds, and felt he could make his meaning clear if in close touch with his audience, to whom the subject-matter would be unfamiliar. His host, a Professor at the University, said he would arrange for the small hall to be used for the second and third lecture, but the first would be in the large hall as many would come to hear him out of curiosity and the numbers were sure to drop for the subsequent lectures. This, it seems, 'always happened to visiting lecturers, however brilliant'. But in the event it was otherwise. The first lecture was sparsely attended—about 600 or 700 people—and the seating capacity, on Jung's estimate, was about 3,000. For the second lecture he presumed he would use the small hall, but he was told that this was impossible, as the large one was already full. At the third lecture the audience had again increased, and there was considerable difficulty in regulating the admission.

After this lecture he was invited to have tea at the Professor's house, and on arrival he was embarrassed to find his hostess weep-

5. *Psychology and Religion: West and East* (1958), C. W. Vol. II, p. 5.

ing. 'I'm sorry,' said Jung. 'Perhaps you are in trouble and I am intruding.' 'Oh, no,' she said. 'There is no trouble.' 'But you are crying.' 'Yes; it was your lectures.' 'But why?' said he. 'Did you not understand what I said? Was I very obscure? It was quite a difficult subject.' 'Oh, no. It wasn't that,' she replied. 'I didn't understand a word of it, but I felt it; it was the way you said it. I felt the truth of what you said, and that is why I am upset.' 'That's it,' Jung remarked in recalling the incident. 'She was "in it".'

Jung regards his time as of importance; he never wastes it over trivial matters and formalities, but goes straight to the essentials; the direct method marks all his work. His power of concentration is immense. Noise, if there is reason for it, does not disturb him. When his house at Bollingen was being altered, incessant hammering went on daily for weeks, but he adjusted easily to this and scarcely noticed it.

Visitors who want to meet him merely because he is a noted person are not welcomed. He is happy with friends, and with colleagues engaged on special work he is generous of his time and his ideas. He 'gives himself' to those he sees, be they young or old, and they feel at ease because he is interested in them and is always natural and frank. His fund of knowledge is profound and exact, and he is well informed on many subjects outside his professional work. Thus, on drives in the Swiss countryside he would point out the geological formations, the architectural features in different cantons, characteristics of the people and the countryside—not to mention his acquaintance with the culinary capacity of the hotels chosen as stopping places.

Eight universities have recognized Jung's original contributions by conferring upon him their honorary degrees, and he is an Honorary Fellow of the Royal Society of Medicine (London). Because of a passing illness in 1960, to his regret he had to decline two invitations: to speak of his work at the Tercentenary Celebration in London of the Royal Society, and, secondly, to take part in the commemorative ceremony marking the anniversary of the foundation, in 1460, of Basel University, his own *alma mater.*

CHAPTER TWO

Impressions of Jung's Childhood and Youth

CARL GUSTAV JUNG, born 1875, was six months old when his father, a parson in the Swiss Reformed Church, moved from the village of Kesswil to the Rhine Fall near Schaffhausen; there, within sight and sound of the waterfall, was his home, adjoining the little church. Before his birth there had been two children, boys, who died as infants, so Carl Gustav was an only child till he was nine, when a sister was born. He was left very much to himself, but he had plenty of interests at home. Following the Swiss custom, he attended the local school, and he enjoyed the companionship of the neighbouring boys and girls, who were mainly the children of peasants from the farms. Jung maintains that his early contact with country boys gave him a balanced view of what are usually called the facts of life. Such matters are to a large extent taken for granted in country places, and he was quite surprised later on, when he met Freud, to find sexual matters given so much importance.

His father, an Oriental and classical scholar, taught him Latin from the age of six, and this produced an appreciation of the classics for which he has always been grateful. Throughout his life he has been able to read Latin texts with ease, and later on medieval Latin had no terrors for him.

Visitors to the famous Rhine Fall passed his father's church and the pastor's house beside it, where, eighty years ago, Jung's early years were spent—not very eventfully so far as external circumstances go. But inwardly they were important, and the impression of certain experiences never completely faded.

One of these, a dream he had at the age of four, had a lasting influence; the memory of it has remained vivid—as vivid as when he had it—and he often thought of it over the years. He dreamt he was alone in the field beside their home where he usually played, when to his surprise he noticed a square hole in the ground. Filled with curiosity, he looked into the hole and saw a flight of stone steps; down these he went slowly, with hesitation. At the bottom was a door covered with a green curtain, which he pulled aside. To his amazement, he saw a large, rectangular room with stone walls; a strip of red carpet stretched from the door to the opposite end, where there was a dais with steps, and upon it a big chair. It was not an ordinary chair, but a large golden throne with a red cushion, and on it rested what he took to be a tree trunk about twelve feet high. This had a red fleshy top, a sort of head, yet not shaped as a head, with an opening like the eye of a demonic god. He had never before seen such a thing and had no idea what it could be, but he felt a strong wave of panic. Then he heard his mother calling to him. Her voice was quite clear, as though she were at the entrance to the steps in the field, yet he realized—in the dream—that she was in the house about 200 yards away. 'Just look at him,' she said. 'He is the Man-eater.' Here the dream ended. He could not understand the dream at all. Suddenly it occurred to him that, as this room was below the surface, so there was in life something mysterious and important in addition to the more ordinary experiences. Church services, his father's talk of an invisible yet powerful God, and all such things had the same quality as this underground room—that is, they were different from everyday happenings, a veiled background of life.

Jung described this astonishing experience as a momentous event. At the time of the dream he felt he must not speak of it; he never did mention it till he was sixty-five years of age, when he related it to his wife, and the silence was next broken when he told it to me.

In this typically introverted attitude towards the dream there is response to an inner situation, to the powerful influence of the unconscious, even though the dream itself was incomprehensible. Naturally, there was no speculation about the dream at the time, for the mind of the child is not encumbered with critical reflection. It would be the height of absurdity to attempt to explain the dream as due to some current event. Impressive dreams of this type come spontaneously from the unconscious and may have no connection with current events; but the effect is immediate and carries its own conviction, apart altogether from conscious understanding. Such dreams occur in childhood, for the child is still close to the world from which it came—the primordial world of the unconscious.

Years later he got glimpses of what the dream meant. Thus in adolescence when his own physical development came he realized that the mysterious object on the cushion, like and unlike a tree trunk, might be a phallus. When first he saw it, he knew that it was of flesh; now he knew what it was. But not fully, for it was only in later years that he recognized it as the phallic archetype, the principle of creativity which is expressed in many forms, such as the resurrection of life, the minaret, the pillar-like grave monuments in Turkey, Assam, and elsewhere, the towers on churches and so on. Until the latter part of the nineteenth century, when prudery reached a zenith, there was a phallus in stone at one of the old gates in Basel. But it was not thought 'proper' and was removed.

Another impressive experience of childhood remained clearly in Jung's mind and, like the dream, was often recalled in the intervening years. It occurred at about the same time and had some of the mysterious quality of the underground-room dream, for it, too, was associated in his mind with his father's allusions to prayer and similar matters, which always seemed to belong to a world apart. Looking out of the window one day, he caught sight of a tall woman walking along the road towards their house and the waterfall. Because of the long dress, he took it for granted that the figure was a woman, but as it came nearer he realized that it was a man wearing a broad hat, and a cloak reaching down to the ground. Naturally, he assumed that the man was disguised, and this added to the mystery. Often he had heard his father talking to friends of Jesuit priests and their sinister doctrines, and he knew the Jesuit

Order was forbidden in Switzerland. It flashed into his mind that this was a Jesuit priest. Living in a Protestant district he had never seen such a person and, being terrified lest the priest would come into their house, he dashed upstairs and hid in the attic. One reason for his alarm was the association of Christ with funerals, and of His taking the dead to Himself; in his mind *Jesuit* was equivalent to *Jesus*. After almost two hours had passed, he descended cautiously to the first floor and peeped from the window. The figure had gone. Of course, the Jesuit priest—if indeed he was a Jesuit wearing his soutane—was merely a visitor to the Rhine Fall. From what he had heard, he believed that all Jesuits were concerned with deep, mysterious, nefarious events, and this incident, with the dream of the underground chamber, remained in his mind as a single, unforgettable event.

When Jung was about eight or nine, an unusual episode had a marked effect upon him. In Basel, a few miles from his home, he saw an ancient, horse-drawn coach with the rococo, gilded body slung between the wheels on broad straps. This was not an unusual sight in those days, for the coach came from the Black Forest, where people were still living, as he expressed it, 'in the eighteenth century, just as my own parents still belonged to the Middle Ages'. As he looked at the coach it was strangely familiar, as if he really knew it; and, in addition, he was aware of a personal bond with the coach and with the period to which it belonged as if he, too, belonged to that time. Thus, as well as being a boy of his own age, he felt as though he were also a child of the eighteenth century. This completely novel notion struck him the moment he saw the coach. It produced no alarm or distress of mind, but rather interest and quiet pleasure. At the time the experience was not recognized as a mixture of fact and fancy, for his reflections were to him as actual as the coach itself. Naturally, he did not understand the experience, but, as any child of that age would do, he accepted it just as it came and made no attempt to comprehend it.

In the same context, he mentioned seeing in the house of a relative two statuettes, one of a man wearing buckled shoes. These shoes fascinated him; he seemed to recognize that type of shoe in a particularly personal way. As with the coach, so with the figure of the man (which belonged to the eighteenth century); he was conscious of an affinity with the period, as though he and it had something in common.

These experiences—the coach and the statuettes—reinforced the ill-defined notion that, although he was a boy of four or five years old, living at the end of the nineteenth century, he felt at the same time that he was a person in the earlier age of, say, the eighteenth century, or at any rate that he had a close bond with this earlier age. This in no way diminished the reality of his present existence, but it enlarged his outlook, so that life became more interesting and happier.

There is, of course, nothing remarkable about this type of experience. But the mixture of intuition and reality—given in explanation of such experiences of duality—is not entirely satisfactory, because it leaves out of account the vivid feeling of being alive in the past, belonging to it. Perhaps in these boyhood experiences lie the germs of his theory of the collective unconscious, for the mind, like the body, has its ancestry.

At about the age of ten, Jung was in the habit of sitting upon a boulder in the garden, and he recalls that from time to time he would fall into a sort of meditation and questioning, such as 'Who am I? I could say I am sitting on the stone, but the stone could say I am supporting him'. Then would come the question: 'Am I myself or am I the stone that supports my weight?' This early reminiscence hints at the experience described by Lévy-Bruhl as 'participation mystique'—that is, the unconscious personality merges with the environment. Jung regrets that Lévy-Bruhl gave up the adjective 'mystique', for it is just the right word to characterize the peculiar quality of 'unconscious' identity, a well-known psychological and psychopathological phenomenon.[1]

A later experience, having marked differences and at the same time some similarity in feeling to the two episodes mentioned above, occurred at the age of eleven or twelve, during a holiday by

1. *Psychology and Religion: West and East*, C. W., Vol II, pp. 221, 504 n.

the Lake of Lucerne. Jung had gone out with the son of his host in a boat—in itself a great thrill—and in an effort to row in the standing position often used in Switzerland, he stood up on the stern. The owner of the boat had warned him before of such pranks, and when he saw him he called him back and 'gave me hell'. But Jung knew at the time he was safe and said to himself, 'What business is it of his? What has he got to do with me; how dare he tell me to be careful? I am an adult man, fully able to look after myself!' He was quite surprised at his own words, for he knew he was only a boy of eleven or twelve; yet in that moment he felt himself to be a grown-up man, and so the scolding seemed to him quite out of place.

After the family moved to Basel and when he was about twelve, Jung entered the Gymnasium, the school for classical teaching, and found himself far ahead of his contemporaries: the early training in Latin was bearing fruit. Often he was idle as the class laboured over Latin grammar; his teacher, to relieve this monotony, would send him to get books from the University library, and he used to linger, absorbed in the old books. Unhurried permeation suited him, for even in those days he disliked a settled programme, being accustomed to make his plans in his own way.

Jung's mother found life as the wife of a country parson rather difficult: her education was much wider than was normal in those days, and, looking back, Jung thought she must have been terribly bored. His father, a friendly man with a happy disposition, enjoyed chatting to his parishioners and got on well with everyone; but he frittered away his time in trivialities, little events of no importance, and let his considerable ability go to seed. At the University he had shown promise of a career as a Hebrew scholar. But all this came to an end on the death of his father (C. G. J.'s grandfather), for the family found themselves short of money and it looked as if this gifted student must take up remunerative work. Then a relative died unexpectedly, leaving a sum of money for the education of any member of the family who wished to become a clergyman. Mainly as a way out of his financial difficulty, Jung's father accepted the legacy and turned to the study of theology; in due course he was ordained. When it came to marriage, his choice fell on the daughter of his old teacher of Hebrew.

Jung found his mother an enigma because she was so unpredictable. On one occasion she told him that he was a disgrace to the family: he was always untidy, with torn, unbrushed clothes and dirty hands. She wanted to be proud of him, for he was then the only child, and she thought to stir him up by comparing him unfavourably with the children of a neighbour, who were always clean, and 'wore nice little gloves and beautiful clothes with bits of lace on the cuffs, altogether admirable!' He was irritated with these wonderful children, and when he got the chance he 'beat them up'. Their mother then appeared and complained to his mother! There was quite a row: 'How could you be so rough and cruel to those nice, well-behaved children?' But a little later, as she was knitting, she lapsed into quiet talking to herself—a habit she had—and he heard her liken these children to a litter of puppies which ought to be destroyed as mongrels. At once he challenged her: 'But you praised them before, and now you say they are like a litter of puppies which ought to be drowned.' She denied it hotly: 'You're a dreadful boy to say such things of your mother.' 'But you did say it yourself. I heard you,' he retorted. But she would not accept this, and continued to blame him. Little by little he came to think she was a rather peculiar, uncertain person. It was all most puzzling for him.

I asked if sports and races were usual when he was at school. There were no such activities then, he told me, so he did not develop an interest in games and similar contests; they never seemed worth while. He had often observed that those who set store by petty triumphs appear to have an inner knowledge that life holds nothing for them; they seek trivial prizes so that at any rate they will have something out of life. Jung was never interested in such insignificant feats. He mentioned a fellow student, a promising scientific worker, who was always taking unnecessary risks in the mountains in order to distinguish himself, to make his mark in this way. Years later he met this man, who by then had retired and was spending his days pottering about his garden, with no interest in his earlier research. Jung always felt (unconscious knowledge) that life held much for him, that he was, as it were, a trustee of something which could be done; that was why after the age of fifteen he refused to take foolish and unnecessary risks.

About the age of twelve, Jung had an impressive dream, and at the time he knew it marked an important change in his outlook. It was perhaps the most significant dream in his whole life. Like that of the underground chamber, it remained clear and fresh in his mind.

This is the dream: 'I was in the rather gloomy courtyard of the Gymnasium at Basel, a beautiful medieval building. From the courtyard I went through the big entrance where the coaches used to come in, and there before me was the Cathedral of Basel, the sun shining on the roof of coloured tiles, recently renovated, a most impressive sight. Above the Cathedral God was sitting on His throne. I thought: "How beautiful it all is! What a wonderful world this is—how perfect, how complete, how full of harmony." Then something happened, so unexpected and so shattering that I woke up. There the dream ended. I could not allow myself to *think* of what I had seen,' he continued, 'for had I done so I would be compelled to accept it, and this I couldn't possibly do. So I made every effort to put the thought from my mind.' (In an aside he remarked: 'So I knew from experience what leads to repression!') 'I lay in bed, unable to get to sleep again, thinking of the dream and of the horrifying picture I had seen. The next day I looked worried and pale, and my mother asked if there was anything wrong: "Has something gone wrong in school?" "Oh, no," I replied. "Everything is all right." ' On the following night the same unwelcome line of thought returned. Yet he could not bring himself to dwell upon what he termed the terrible part of the dream; he turned from it with a shudder. At that time he was a firm believer in the Christian teaching given by his father about Christ, sin, forgiveness, and other doctrines. If he allowed himself, now fully awake, to think the thought he had had in the dream or to look again at what he had seen in the dream, it would be the 'unforgivable sin'. But on the third night he reflected: 'Perhaps God wants me to think this thing as a test, to see if I am a true believer. But,' he thought, 'where could such an awful thing come from? Could it come from the Devil? But then the Devil would be greater than God.' Then came the idea: 'God is testing me, and if I could accept the awful thought it would prove my belief in God. Where could it possibly come from? Perhaps from my father? That is impossible, for he is a true believer. Nor could it have come from my mother; that, too, is impossible, for she would never think such things. Then perhaps from my grandfather? But he was a Professor of Medicine, and he wouldn't be likely to have such thoughts. Possibly the awful thought came from my maternal grandfather? Yet he held a high position in the Church. Certainly he could never have thought such a shameful thing.' It occurred to him that a possible source of the terrible thought must be in the distant past; it might have come even from the Fall of Adam. But that was too far away, too abstract. All his pondering was quite inconclusive. Then came a great moment: he sat up in bed, sweating and trembling, for he felt: 'God must mean me to accept this awful scene as my own thought,' and at that moment he did accept it. It was as follows: From his throne God 'dropped' a vast fæces on the Cathedral and smashed it to pieces. This was a terrific thing, for it could only mean that the Church, his father's teaching, and his own beliefs had to be thought of in an entirely different way, because God had poured scorn on every one of them.[2]

Acceptance of the dream as a fact had a marked influence on Jung, resembling in some ways the impression produced by the incident at Lucerne,[3] but much more impressive. He was conscious of a calm assurance that he was now a person in his own right. Tension

2. Dr. Adler kindly pointed out to me that in the autobiography, referred to in the Preface, Jung implied that this episode was a vision and not a dream. When Jung first recounted the experience to me, on January 3rd, 1957, he spoke of it as a highly important *dream*. We discussed the subject on later occasions and Jung continued to use the term dream, which also occurred in the typescript of this book which Jung read. But there need be no confusion between the terms vision and dream, for there is no essential difference between them; both are natural products of the unconscious. Jung writes: '. . . a vision is in the last resort nothing less than a dream which has broken through into the waking state'.
3. See p. 14.

and anxiety about the dream faded, and so did all the disturbing ideas that he was two people,[4] divided in some unfamiliar way by opposing thoughts. Probably these sprang from identification with his father, for this could bring uncertainty about his personal identity. Now he knew: 'I am I; I must be myself; I must think for myself; I must admit only what *I* understand.' Here was an unequivocal experience, accepted unhesitatingly as his own.

This may sound a trifle sententious for a boy of twelve; but young adolescents can take life very seriously, yet without a trace of pomposity. It only appears sententious or pompous from the standpoint of the adult, perhaps the slightly cynical or condescending adult. Anyhow, for Jung it was a great event, and one never to be doubted.

Jung has always acknowledged the influence of these early and intimate personal events upon his life. What took place within his own mind—in dreams, for instance—has been more significant than external circumstances. This is what might be expected, for he has the psychology of the introverted thinker, and his reflections are often stimulated in ways that to someone else would be meaningless. Facts observed by another will be observed also by Jung, but he may derive entirely different conclusions from these facts. This does not imply a quality of uniqueness in Jung, but illustrates how introverted thinking proceeds. From early life his predominant interest has been the inner value, and so the importance of an incident lies in his reaction to it, for this makes an inevitable contribution to his comprehension of the external happening. Perhaps his thoughts in childhood, evoking as they did an immediate inner response, foreshadowed the concept of autonomy in the unconscious. Naturally, the predominantly extraverted thinker will find this rather high-flown, esoteric; but for others it will be simple, even trite common sense. With the best will in the world, the extravert, whatever his functional type, will find Jung's books hard going.

From the Gymnasium Jung went on to the University of Basel, where his grandfather had been Professor of Medicine and where

4. See p. 12.

later on he himself was to become Professor of Psychiatry. Although he had distinct leanings towards archaeology, he joined the natural science class, but later changed to medicine. He was keen to learn, but he must have been a rather trying student, because he was constantly asking questions in class. When taught about the ether, he questioned its existence, saying it was merely a guess, a theory with little foundation. Some teachers thought him stupid and silly to have ideas of his own. But, nothing daunted, he continued with his problems. It is to be noted that this confident manner was relatively new, for it dated from the dream of Basel Cathedral. That a dream could have such an effect will surprise only those who have never had a 'big dream'. It didn't surprise Jung at the time; it was accepted much as a child accepts the fact that he can walk, as a youth accepts the fact that he can swim. He needed no proof, for the dream carried its own credentials.

Professor Lewis,[5] in a comprehensive article, surveys the work published by Jung between 1902 and 1907, while at the Burghölzli Hospital. He adds reflectively: 'I do not know what occupied his interest before he went to the Burghölzli in 1900—passing his medical examinations, I suppose.' Jung did pass his examinations without any difficulty. They were taken in his stride. But in addition his interest was largely directed to subjects beyond the everyday routine of a medical student. One experience, at first glance trivial, turned out to be most important in the shaping of his career. He and a few young friends, the children of neighbours, were trying to make something of table-rapping and similar things. To their amazement, one of the group, a girl of fifteen, went into a trance and began to talk in high German in a stilted fashion, altogether different from her ordinary voice and language, for, like the others, she was accustomed to speak colloquial Swiss German. Thinking over this incident, Jung was struck by the complexity of the human mind, and saw it as one might observe any phenomenon, whereas till then he had taken the mind for granted. His companions found the incident

5. Lewis, Sir, Aubrey, 'Jung's Early Work', *Journal of Analytical Psychology* (1957), II, p. 119.

quite entertaining, and so did he. But he went further, and asked himself: 'What is happening below the surface in this girl's mind?'

He was fascinated by this novel problem, and at subsequent sessions Jung, in his systematic manner, took full notes of what the girl said. Some years later he used these as a thesis for his M.D. degree, and an expanded version of this has been published, first in 1902 and recently in the *Collected Works*.[6] Anyone reading the finished essay without knowing the history of it might easily miss the significance of this early incident.

About 1896 or 1897 a fellow student invited him to visit his home in Schaffhausen for a couple of days. While glancing at the books in the library, he came upon one on spiritualism, mesmerism, and such topics published years before. At the time he knew nothing of these subjects, and saw at once that they might have a bearing on the strange behaviour of the girl who had fallen into a trance. But while his curiosity was aroused and he studied the literature of spiritualism and similar subjects, searching for some light on the girl's unusual state of mind, the answer eluded him. Much later—about 1900—he chanced to read the introduction to a book by Krafft-Ebing, and it was through this that he saw the possibility of uniting medicine with philosophical interests. There and then Jung decided to make psychiatry his career.

He tells us that this girl led a curiously contradictory life, a real double life, with two personalities existing side by side or in succession, each continually striving for mastery. One was that of the girl of fifteen; the other that of a clever and mature woman. Very soon she took up dressmaking and dress-designing, and she developed unusually quickly. By the age of twenty-two she had established herself in business and was employing over twenty assistants. Her work was of a high order; she made the most beautiful designs for dresses and in every way was a brilliant success. In addition she won a reputation as a medium and many people were interested in her. On one occasion—this was later on—Jung discovered that she was cheating. She had claimed to be in a trance, but he suspected that

6. *Psychiatric Studies* (1975), C. W., Vol. 1, p. 17.

she was playacting, and told her so, and she admitted that she was not in a trance at all. He had nothing more to do with her after this. Her reputation had become too much for her; she could not keep up with it, so she used pretence.

Apart from this, she did present a remarkable phenomenon, described in detail by Jung. In the early experiments she was not cheating, and she spoke and acted as though she had two personalities. Jung got an impression that unconsciously she knew that her life would be short, and consequently she telescoped her future personality into that of the immature girl. There was no indication in her early twenties or in her teens that her health was anything but sound; nevertheless, she contracted consumption and died after a long illness at the age of twenty-six.

CHAPTER THREE

Experience at the Burghölzli Hospital

EUGEN BLEULER, Professor of Psychiatry in the University of Zürich, was Director of the Burghölzli Hospital when Jung joined his staff in 1900. A progressive atmosphere had been built up, and Jung found his colleagues very much to his taste: they were well informed, keen, and enthusiastic. His immediate senior on the staff suggested that he should do research on sections of brain tissue in the expectation that some pathological condition would prove to be the cause of mental illness, particularly dementia praecox. Jung had taken up psychiatry determined to discover 'the intruders of the mind', as he described abnormal ideas—that is, the disturbing delusions and hallucinations. Microscopic examination of brain tissue was entirely new to him, and he began it hoping for great results. Sometimes the professor gave him the responsibility for a course of lectures in general physiology. But his research work was in vain; it threw no light on the problems of causation and treatment, which were his main objectives, and so it was abandoned.

At that time hypnotism was passing through one of its cycles of popularity, and it was quite the vogue at the Burghölzli. Bleuler's predecessor, August Forel, was a noted writer on the subject. Three stages were described, and this threefold division was thought to be highly important; but, as is well known, Forel's so-called stages of hypnosis were later regarded as entirely artificial.

Jung did a great deal of hypnotic treatment at the Burghölzli, but he grew very tired of it as it explained nothing and he felt he was working in the dark. Nevertheless, he was in charge of the hypnotism clinic for a time; like everyone else, he got plenty of symptomatic cures, and the value of these was fully recognized. But his aim was to find out the meaning of the illness—to understand rather that obliterate the symptoms. What had changed a previously happy person into a depressed, deluded, anti-social invalid? Hypnotism provided no answer to such a problem.

Although Forel had retired, hypnotism was still used in the hospital and there were many stories current about his work. It was said that he used to collect a group of patients, tell them in an authoritative way to go to sleep and, when everyone was sleeping or pretending to do so, he would leave them. But after he had gone they would chat together—which probably helped them a lot—till they heard his step in the corridor, and, of course, all were sleeping correctly when he walked in.

A serious drawback to hypnotic treatment—so Jung felt—was the withdrawal of initiative from the patient, and this, by the way, was one of his later criticisms of Freud's psychoanalysis: the patient became too passive and left everything to the doctor. In those early days Jung was impressed by Freud's writings, and he was one of the few who recognized his qualities. For the most part, Freud received little or no attention. He, too, had used hypnosis and found it lacking. Sometimes it has been suggested that he gave it up because he was unable to hypnotize obsessional patients. Jung told me this was not the case, and that Freud abandoned hypnosis because he found it superficial and often disappointing, savouring more of magic than of medicine.

Over and above his other work, Jung spent a great deal of time talking to patients in the wards in the hope that he might discover something about the onset of their illnesses and find out, if he could, what the symptoms meant to them. Although the results varied, he learnt a great deal by direct contact with the patients. One of several patients with whom he concerned himself particularly was an elderly woman who had been in the hospital almost forty years—so long that none of the nurses remembered her arrival, and they had come to accept her as just another senile patient. She had an odd habit of moving her hands up and down, and she 'shovelled' the food into her mouth with this movement. The students saw her in demonstrations as an example of dementia praecox, catatonic type, and that was all, for there was no psychological point of view in those days. One evening, when going round the ward, Jung asked an older nurse if she knew any details about the patient's early history. Information was scant, but the nurse recalled that many years ago she had been told that the patient had had some connection with shoe-making, but, as the patient had never spoken since she had known her, there was no information about her early life. It dawned on Jung that the movements of her hands resembled the action of cobblers in country districts. Eventually the patient died and her brother came to the hospital. Jung asked him why his sister had come to the asylum. 'Ah!' he replied. 'She was going to marry a shoemaker, but he jilted her and she went mad.' To Jung it seemed possible that the ideas and associations of long ago lived on in the hand movements. This record has a special interest, for his observations and reflections about this patient gave him the idea of a possible psychogenic element in dementia praecox.

Doctors from outside Switzerland were attracted to the Burghölzli in the early days of this century through the publications of Jung and other members of the staff. One of these by Jung and a colleague, Dr. W. F. Peterson,[1] must be among the first psychiatric contributions to show that the influence of emotion can be demonstrated physiologically as well as psychologically.

A similar psychophysical relation was shown again and again in the experiments connected with what was known as the 'association method', a procedure used extensively before Jung's time by workers in experimental psychology, and chiefly by Darwin's kinsman, Sir Francis Galton. Here the procedure was to read a series of words to the test subject, who had been instructed to answer as quickly as possible with the word which came into his

1. "Psycho-physical Investigations with the Galvanometer and Pneumograph in Normal and Insane Individuals', *Brain*, XXX (1907), pp. 118, 153–218.

mind. With a stop-watch, the tester recorded the reaction time—that is, the delay between hearing the test word and the response. This sounded so simple that it surprised Jung and his colleagues when patient after patient, many of them intelligent and fluent, experienced difficulty in carrying out the simple instruction of giving an immediate response. How was this to be explained? Originally the test was devised to distinguish certain intellectual types, and for this it proved of little value. But, as Jung was the first to demonstrate, the responses to the test depended on the emotions, not on the intellectual qualities of the person tested. Often the rate of heartbeat and respiration, and at times the psycho-galvanic reaction, were recorded, in addition to the verbal response to the stimulus word. A graph of such a test showed a correspondence between the verbal response, the respiration rate, and the psycho-galvanic effect. In other words, the mind and body acted as a unit; there were no separated functions. An account of the association method appeared in English in 1920, and is referred to elsewhere in Jung's published work.[2] Professor A. C. Mace of London University, speaking at a function in honour of Professor Jung's eightieth birthday, referred to Jung's work on the association method, and, with permission, an extract from his speech is given here:

'There is a strange, but I think significant, resemblance between the way in which the spirit of religion tends to become petrified and imprisoned in ritual and dogma, and the way in which the spirit of science is apt to be enslaved to methodology and technique. This is what happened to Galton's psychometric studies and to his lively explorations of human personality. The investigation of word-association was reduced to a tedious laboratory procedure. Instruments were designed to measure association-times to a thousandth of a second, and refined statistical techniques were devel-

2. *Collected Papers on Analytical Psychology*, Baillière, Tindall, and Cox (1920), p. 94. Attention is also drawn to a chapter entitled 'A Review of the Complex Theory' in *The Structure and Dynamics of the Psyche* (1960), C. W., Vol. 8, p. 92.

oped for revealing "significant" but uninteresting differences. In his *Studies in Word Association*, Jung showed that he could play the Laboratory Game as well as any of the rest, *and* that he could do so without any sacrifice of the interest in content to the interest in method. In the results of these remarkable experiments we can see how near Galton had been to making great discoveries. Galton had noted the similarity of associations of men with a common cultural background, and in his studies of twins he had shown how much alike in the minutest detail the thoughts of twins can be. But the full significance of these facts was first made clear by Jung who rescued these studies from scientific pedantry and reinvested them with the vitality and interest of real life.'

Two important results came from these experiments, and the study of the method and its issues became a feature in the teaching of the Zürich School. First was Jung's theory of the complex, and, secondly, the striking fact that the responses to the tests were quite apart from consciousness; in other words, the response was autonomous, the complex behaved, so to speak, on its own, independently of the conscious wishes or ideas of the subject.

Delays and mistakes occurred when the test word touched on certain ideas, and a constellation of this nature was described as an 'emotionally toned complex', later abbreviated to 'complex'.

There has been some confusion about the word 'complex' because at one time Jung employed it to describe a constellation either of conscious or of unconscious ideas. For many years now, however, the notion of the conscious complex has been superseded, and in current use complex means a group of ideas repressed from the control of consciousness—that is to say, autonomous complexes which can only be brought once more into conscious control by analysis, or some other method designed to overcome the resistance of the unconscious. Jung speaks of ' . . . this dark side of the soul [that] does not come within the purview of consciousness, and therefore the patient cannot deal with it, correct it, resign himself to it, or renounce it, for he cannot be said to *possess* [i.e. be in control of] the unconscious impulses. By being repressed from the hierarchy of the conscious soul, they have become *autonomous complexes* which can be brought again under control by analysis of the unconscious, though not without great resistance.'[3]

How can the effect of the complex be explained? It behaved like a partial or splinter personality with the result that the subject acted and thought as though disturbed by someone else or by external circumstances. But this was impossible, for there was no second person; so, inevitably, it was assumed that the interference came from within, from the unconscious, and came spontaneously, apart from will. Its occurrence surprised the patient as much as the testers. Jung considered Janet's explanation: that dissociation was caused by a rise and fall of psychical tension. But this was a description rather than an explanation. There were other objections to Janet's theory: the complex appeared to function with considerable strength, and this was not compatible with a psychasthenic condition, which is, by definition, a state of weakened psychical tension. After prolonged discussion and personal reflection, Jung reached the conclusion that the most satisfactory and the most probable explanation was Freud's theory of repression.

Jung, as we have seen, was familiar with Freud's work. He had been attracted to it in the first instance because Freud accorded importance to the mind itself, and did not regard it merely as a nebulous entity, vaguely associated with the body. Consequently, he wrote to Freud telling him of the experimental confirmation of his theory of repression. He also pointed out the striking feature that the complex behaved autonomously. Freud was naturally interested to hear from Jung, and appreciated the importance of his conclusion, for Jung's reputation was then established, and his name would certainly have been known to Freud. Freud expressed his interest in the autonomous nature of the complex, but, strange to say, he made no use of this fact.

Although Jung has not employed the association method for many years, it constituted a significant step in his thinking and opened the way for future developments. The conclusions it was

3. *Collected Papers on Analytical Psychology*, Baillière, Tindall, and Cox (1920), p. 377.

possible to draw from the results of many tests—on individuals and in groups—impressed Jung very much, and they were the first steps which led eventually to his throwing in his lot with Freud.

It was as a complex-indicator that the test became well known, and it came in for a lot of criticism. It was argued, for instance, that in some cases the test word touched on conscious material and therefore could have nothing to do with a complex, which is unconscious. Such a question is based on a misunderstanding. These tests were used to contact what Jung later described as the 'personal unconscious', which contains material previously conscious. Consequently, the contents of the personal unconscious are qualitatively the same as consciousness and might just as well be conscious; in fact, the individual may be unconscious of a thing at one time and conscious of it at another.

We may be unconscious of the answer to a question during an examination, although it had been known to us earlier, and it may return to consciousness later, probably when we have left the examination hall! By asking a person, we can decide whether a particular content is or is not conscious at a certain time. If it is not conscious, then it is repressed or forgotten—that is, unconscious. But it has not ceased to exist; although unconscious, its effect in the test is plain to see.

Jung rightly took it for granted that the results of the tests were facts. Information not previously known to the doctor or to the patient, in these circumstances, became available. Extensive use was made of the method in practical psychological work, in medico-legal work, in analysis, and in investigating interfamily relationships by giving the test to members of the same family. This research proved valuable. The reader will find ample details in Jung's writings.[4]

It has been observed that the attitude of the subject towards the test affected the result. Some subjects assumed that they were having an intelligence test or that a method was being used to take an indiscreet look behind the scenes, as Jung puts it.[5] The disturbance

4. *Ibid.*, p. 119.
5. *The Structure and Dynamics of the Psyche* (1960), C. W., Vol. 8, p. 93.

took place consciously and could invalidate the accuracy of the results, or of some of them. Such complications had previously been regarded as failures to react. Nevertheless, the presence of these side-effects showed that there were no isolated psychic processes, or at any rate no means had yet been found of demonstrating them experimentally. 'The unspoken background'[6] was revealed by reaction disturbances, and this is comparable to the situation that takes place when two people have a discussion. In the complex, therefore, we find 'a psychic factor which, in terms of energy, possesses a value that often exceeds our conscious intentions.'[7]

It was somewhat cumbersome and rather impersonal to read lists of words, using a stop-watch and making calculations, and some workers, including Jung, found it boring. This led to inaccuracy, for the attitude of the tester reacted on the test subject. Then, again, some patients took it too seriously and others too frivolously, so in several ways it had limitations. As a complex-indicator it had its place. But that was only a first step. Jung found that it interfered with the doctor-patient relationship, so he used it less and less, and finally dropped it altogether.

In 1906 Jung published *The Psychology of Dementia Praecox*. This was translated into English by the late Dr. A. A. Brill,[8] who visited the hospital in 1907. In his Introduction, Brill refers to the ardent and enthusiastic workers at the Burghölzli, and particularly to Jung, who was the leading spirit in the work on the word association tests. An added interest in the experiments was to discover if Freud's views on repression were confirmed, and, as we know, the results supported the soundness of Freud's theory.[9] Brill considered that Jung's book on dementia praecox was the only work of its kind to give a résumé of the problem of this illness, and adds: 'there is no question that next to Freud's case it forms the cornerstone of modern interpretative psychiatry'. *The Psychology of Dementia Praecox*

6. *The Structure and Dynamics of the Psyche* (1960), C. W., Vol. 8, p. 95.
7. *Ibid.*, p. 96.
8. *The Psychology of Dementia Praecox*, trans. A. A. Brill, Nervous and Mental Disease Publishing Co. (1936).
9. See p. 28.

established Jung's reputation, and even today, more than fifty years later, the book holds its place.

Jung's interest in the psychology of schizophrenia has been maintained throughout his career. In 1939 he read a paper, 'On the Psychogenesis of Schizophrenia', before the Psychiatric Section of the Royal Society of Medicine.[10] At the Second International Congress of Psychiatry, held at Zürich in 1957, Jung contributed a paper on 'Schizophrenia',[11] in which he traces the growth of his thought from 1901 to 1958 on the still mysterious disorder, schizophrenia. But the paper is more than a historical survey, for while reference is made to earlier views, it gives later ideas, and chiefly his acceptance of the possibility of development in new measures that might prove valuable in determining the aetiology and treatment of schizophrenia: 'Despite, however, the undoubted psychogeneity of most cases, which would lead one to expect the disease to run a purely psychological course, schizophrenia exhibits concomitant phenomena that do not seem to me to be explicable psychologically. . . . It will assuredly be a long time before the physiology and pathology of the brain and the psychology of the unconscious are able to join hands. Till then they must go their separate ways. But psychiatry, whose concern is the total man, is forced by its task of understanding and treating the sick to consider both sides, regardless of the gulf that yawns between the two aspects of the psychic phenomenon.'

In a brief Appendix to this paper, Jung, writing of schizophrenia, adds: 'But it was just my psychological approach that led me to the hypothesis of a chemical factor, without which I would not be able to explain certain pathognomonic details in its symptomatology. I arrived at the chemical hypothesis by a process of psychological elimination rather than by specifically chemical research. . . . to make myself clear, I consider the aetiology of schizophrenia to be a dual one: namely up to a certain point psychology is indispensable

10. *The Psychogenesis of Mental Disease* (1960), C.W., Vol. 3, p. 233 (previously published in the *Journal of Mental Science* (1939), LXXXV, p. 999).
11. *Ibid.*, pp. 256, 268, 271, 272.

in explaining the nature and the causes of the initial emotions which give rise to metabolic alterations. These emotions seem to be accompanied by chemical processes that cause specific temporary or chronic disturbances or lesions.'

In the Preface Jung expresses his appreciation of Freud: 'Even a superficial glance at my work will show how much I am indebted to the brilliant discoveries of Freud. . . . In the beginning I naturally entertained all the objections that are customarily made against Freud in the literature. . . . Fairness to Freud, however, does not imply, as many fear, unqualified submission to a dogma; one can very well maintain an independent judgment. If I, for instance, acknowledge the complex mechanisms of dreams and hysteria, this does not mean that I attribute to the infantile sexual trauma the exclusive importance that Freud apparently does. Still less does it mean that I place sexuality so predominantly in the foreground or that I grant it the psychological universality which Freud, it seems, postulates in view of the admittedly enormous rôle which sexuality plays in the psyche. . . . Nevertheless, all these things are the merest trifles compared with the psychological principles whose discovery is Freud's greatest merit; and to them the critics pay far too little attention.'[12]

Freud's emphasis on the significance of the instinctual sexual libido or energy surprised Jung. It is perhaps worth repeating that Jung had been brought up in the country, where the breeding of animals and associated matters made the details of sexual life common knowledge. But no one then thought of sexuality as paramount, worthy of being the subject of a dogma. To Jung it seemed nonsense to insist upon a dogma about something everyone took for granted. Nor was sexuality by any means the only form of instinctual energy, let alone the most important; therefore it seemed unscientific as well as too narrow to give it such prominence. But, said Jung, dwellers in Vienna, such as Freud and his pupils, had no notion of primitive conditions where food is the main concern. Anyone with experience

12. *The Psychogenesis of Mental Disease* (1960), C. W. Vol. 3, p. 4.

of Japanese prisoner-of-war camps would agree with Jung's statement, for hunger, continued day by day, will soon displace sexual urges.

Jung's concept of energy is much wider than Freud's, as the following statement shows: 'If we take our stand on the basis of scientific common sense and avoid philosophical considerations which would carry us too far, we would probably do best to regard the psychic process simply as a life-process. In this way we enlarge the narrower concept of psychic energy to a broader one of life-energy which includes "psychic energy" as a specific part. We thus gain the advantage of being able to follow quantitative relations beyond the narrow confines of the psychic into the sphere of biological functions in general, and so can do justice, if need be, to the long discussed and ever-present problem of "mind and body".'[13] Again: 'While I do not connect any specifically sexual definition with the word "libido", this is not to deny the existence of a sexual dynamism any more than any other dynamism, for instance that of the hunger-drive, etc. . . . I therefore expressly declared . . . that the libido with which we operate is not only not concrete or known, but is a complete *x*, a pure hypothesis, a model or counter, and is no more concretely conceivable than the energy known to the world of physics.'[14]

Hence there are two ways in which we are aware of energy: energy on the widest or cosmic plane, and energy as it shows itself in the psychic life of individuals.

Mental energy is a much-debated concept in psychology and in philosophy. Bergson's *élan vital*, for instance, is a specific theory of mental energy and is different from Jung's view. It is mentioned here because the two have been confused. Those who seek a complete exposition of Jung's standpoint are referred to his paper 'On Psychic Energy' from which the above quotations are taken.

Jung objected to what he regarded as Freud's attempt to impose the theory of the sexual libido upon nature. Such an attempt would

13. *The Structure and Dynamics of the Psyche* (1960), C. W., Vol. 8, p. 17.
14. *Ibid.*, p. 30.

be self-limiting and a hindrance rather than a help in understanding nature. By way of illustration, he told the story of a Rabbi and his pupils who went for a walk in the country. Suddenly they came upon a big dog by a farmhouse, and it barked furiously at them. The Rabbi said to his pupils, "Don't be alarmed. Barking dogs never bite.' But the dog drew nearer, barking and snarling, and the Rabbi quickly gathered up his cloak and ran. Later the pupils said, 'Master, why did you run? You told us that barking dogs never bite.' 'Ah, yes! *We* know that barking dogs never bite, but I'm not sure whether the dog knows it too.' There is no point in having a theory which *we* know, but which Nature doesn't know.

CHAPTER FOUR

Jung and Freud: Hail and Farewell

JUNG and his wife visited Freud in Vienna in 1907 and were warmly received. Freud greeted them at their hotel, presented Mrs. Jung with flowers and invited them to his house, where they met his wife and members of the household—the children and Mrs. Freud's sister, who lived with them and helped Freud with secretarial work. There had been correspondence between Freud and the Zürich school, and this visit placed the contact on a personal basis. According to Ernest Jones,[1] Freud saw a risk of psychoanalysis becoming a Jewish racial affair, and as Jung was not a Jew he was all the more welcome to Freud. Recognition from Jung and Bleuler, psychiatrists of established standing, was naturally gratifying to him. 'After so many years of being cold-shouldered, ridiculed and abused, it would have needed an exceptionally philosophical disposition not to have been elated when well-known university teachers from a famous Psychiatric Clinic abroad appeared on the scene in wholehearted support of his work.'[2] This was in 1908.

Jung in his turn was eager to know Freud, and he records that he was the most remarkable person he had then met. Their first talk, in Freud's house, lasted for thirteen hours! For Jung the meeting was a mixture of expectation and disappointment. He hoped for much, but seemed unable to get beyond the confines of Freud's narrow approach, his restricted perspective and concentration on

1. Jones, E., *Sigmund Freud*, Hogarth Press (1955), Vol. II, p. 53.
2. *Ibid.*, p. 48.

tiny details, and his theoretical assumptions. According to Jung, the talk was protracted because he continued to question Freud, hoping to get beyond these limitations, and in particular Freud's insistence on the importance of the infantile sexual trauma as a settled, unalterable basis of his work.

During his stay Jung had a dream: He was in a ghetto, and the place was narrow and twisted, with low ceilings and staircases hanging down. He thought to himself: 'How in hell can people live in such a place?' This came as rather a shock. He could not identify the place with Vienna and, further, so far as he knew, he was happy to be there.

On many topics their outlook conformed—for example, on Freud's valuation of transference. When Freud asked, 'What do you think of transference?' Jung immediately answered, 'It is the alpha and omega in treatment.' 'You have understood,' added Freud. Although Jung's views on transference changed later, he always recognized the brilliance of Freud's original description of transference. Freud's theory of repression had impressed Jung before they met and, notwithstanding statements to the contrary,[3] he has always insisted on the importance of repression.

Here we may anticipate an incident which occurred two years later, when Jung again visited Freud in Vienna. Once more they were in Freud's study talking about the psychoanalytical movement. On many previous occasions Jung had found Freud difficult, but at this meeting he felt, for the first time, that the association was becoming almost impossible, mainly because of Freud's unyielding and—as Jung felt—almost fanatical determination that the movement must develop only on certain lines. During the talk, both were startled by a formidable crash—this is how Jung described it—as if the entire bookcase was coming down. 'What do you make of that?' Jung exclaimed and then, quite spontaneously, added, 'It will happen again'—and it did. They examined the bookcase, but found nothing. Jung knew instantly that this was a parapsychological phenomenon—that is, an expression of a psychic situation. He had read

3. See Glover, E., *Freud or Jung*, George Allen and Unwin (1950), p. 191.

all the available literature on the subject in his effort to understand the mediumistic girl.[4] In his own home in Basel he had experience of at least two similar occurrences. One was when a carving knife split into four pieces with a report like a pistol. Jung was in an adjoining room, and rushed in to find out what was wrong. Apparently everything was in order, but eventually the knife was discovered in the cupboard. Jung showed me the fragments of the knife, and the breaks are quite 'clean'. A second episode was the splitting of an old walnut table that had belonged to his grandmother. Here again there was a loud report. Jung's mother was in the room at the time, but not near the table. He was reading in another room and, as with the knife, hurried in to investigate. Very careful enquiries were made at the time in order to explain these unusual happenings. The knife was examined by a competent cutler and the table by a carpenter. But the mystery remained.

Jung told Freud that they should take the crash seriously; it crossed his mind that there might be a split between them; but, although Freud was aghast, he sneered at the occurrence and refused to give it consideration. Prior to this Vienna visit Jung had spoken to his chief, Bleuler, about these parapsychological phenomena. Bleuler said it was all nonsense; nevertheless, twenty years later he became very much interested in these and similar matters. Such phenomena are often described as exteriorized effects; they do occur, and, like complexes, may be projected. Freud brushed the whole thing aside, but this did not dispose of the matter. Jung does not claim to give an explanation of these undetermined psychic processes, but this is far from saying they do not or could not exist. To prove the negative—that no such events take place—would be a difficult task, and to dismiss them as rubbish, without giving any explanation, is to display ignorance.

Looking back on the bookcase crash Jung can only think of it as a meaningful coincidence—that is, a synchronistic event not explainable in terms of cause and effect.

Jung was astonished and sorry to hear that Ernest Jones had

4. See p. 19.

described the incident of the bookcase as a demonstration given to entertain Freud. Jones writes: 'On one of his first visits to Vienna on March 25, 1909, he [Jung] regaled Freud one evening with astonishing stories of his experiences, and also displayed his powers as a poltergeist by making various articles in the room rattle on the furniture.'[5] Jung did not blame Jones, for he knew from other sources that Freud had told this story, and he thought it likely that Jones had repeated what Freud had said. But the story was not true to the facts. Jung considered it preposterous to describe the episode as a poltergeist phenomenon, and the suggestion that he had caused the cracking was fantastic. 'Freud's memory, like everyone else's, could be treacherous at times.'[6] At the time Jung and Freud took it for granted that the sound was due to inexplicable expansion of the wood of the bookcase, and both were startled and impressed by it. In any event, added Jung, why didn't Ernest Jones ask me about this and other incidents in the early days? He had my address,[7] and as I was the only person still alive who had been there, I could have told him what had happened.

This so-called poltergeist story faded into the background and had no visible effects on the collaboration of Freud and Jung. Its resuscitation appears to date from the era when a section of Freud's followers seemed intent on finding what they considered to be weak points in Jung's work and personality.

Freud was quite familiar with the waywardness of memory and devoted a chapter in *The Psychopathology of Everyday Life* to 'Forgetting of Impressions and Resolutions'. It is unlikely that he attached significance to the incident, and it is not mentioned in his *Autobiographical Study*.

A minor lapse of memory on the part of Jones is the statement that Leonhard Seif broke away from Freud and joined Jung.[8] Jones must have known Seif intimately for he stayed with him at

5. Jones, E., *Sigmund Freud*, Hogarth Press (1957), Vol. III, p. 411.
6. Jones, E., *Sigmund Freud*, Hogarth Press (1953), Vol. I, Preface.
7. See p. 41.
8. Jones E., *Sigmund Freud*, Hogarth Press (1955), Vol. II, p. 97.

Partenkirchen in 1912.[9] Seif himself told me that he had joined Adler, and Jung confirmed this.

A further inaccuracy on the part of Jones, which in fairness to Jung should be mentioned, is his statement that Freud and Ferenczi, when they met Jung at Bremen before the trip to America, persuaded Jung to give up his principle of abstinence and to join them in drinking wine.[10] Jones enlarges on this topic, declaring[11] that Bleuler and Jung never got on well and that Jung thought Bleuler's unfriendly attitude had arisen because he (Jung) had allowed Freud to persuade him to drink alcohol. Jung told me in 1959 that the source of this story was the rule at the Burghölzli, as at other Swiss hospitals, that the medical staff must be teetotal. Jung had taken wine before joining the staff, but he kept loyally to the rule while at the hospital. When he resigned, he resumed his custom of having wine with his meals. That his departure from abstinence had upset Bleuler, Jung described as ridiculous, for he had given up his appointment at the Burghölzli six months before Freud, Ferenczi, and Jung met at Bremen preparatory to their trip to America.

Jones was not on intimate terms with Freud during the period of the Freud-Jung collaboration. He was introduced to Freud, by Jung, in 1908,[12] and in September of the same year he (Jones) took up an appointment at the University of Toronto.[13] His attitude towards Jung in these early days was friendly and appreciative. Thus in 1910[14] he writes about the psychological mechanisms involved in uncovering the repressed complex: 'They have been worked out with great accuracy and detail by Freud and Jung and an exact study of them is essential to the use of the psycho-analytic method. . . . Other means of reaching buried mental complexes may briefly be mentioned. . . . The word-reaction association method as developed by Jung is of the highest assistance, particularly in furnishing us with a series of clues to serve as starting points for future analyses.'

9. *Ibid.*, p. 106.
10. *Ibid.*, p. 61.
11. *Ibid.*, p. 80.
12. *Ibid.*, p. 45.
13. Jones, E., *Free Associations*, Hogarth Press (1959), p. 175.
14. Jones, E., *A Symposium: Psychotherapeutics* (1910), pp. III, 113.

But after the break with Freud a change occurs, and Jones's allusions to Jung become emotionally barbed: 'Two former adherents of Freud—Adler and Jung—after a short period of co-operation, abjured his methods and conclusions and founded independent systems of psychology, which largely consist in denials of Freud's.'[15] 'Abjure' means to renounce on oath, and the use of such a word suggests, not considered judgment, but emotional bias.

In the years following their meeting, Freud and Jung were closely associated, and very understandably this was a cause of offence to Freud's group in Vienna, who felt they were being passed over. Since his separation from Breuer in 1894, Freud worked alone until 1902 or 1903 when a small number of Viennese doctors gathered round him. Being Jews, they were sensitive about the arrival of a non-Jew and assumed Jung would be anti-Semitic. 'It was natural that Freud should make much of his new Swiss followers. . . . his possibly excessive elation was not pleasing to the Viennese. . . . Their jealousy inevitably centred on Jung, about whom Freud was specially enthusiastic. Their attitude was accentuated by their Jewish suspicion of Gentiles in general, with its rarely failing expectation of anti-Semitism. Freud himself shared this to some extent, but for the time being it was dormant in the pleasure of being at last recognized by the outer world.'[16]

Jung was quickly on friendly terms with Freud himself, but he found his medical friends strange, probably because they were entirely different from the medical men he knew in Switzerland. There were few Jews and no anti-Semitism in Switzerland, so he was interested in Freud's pupils, though he did not find them attractive. Ernest Jones[17] writes: 'Jung had told me in Zürich what a pity it was that Freud had no followers of any weight in Vienna, and that he was surrounded there by a "degenerate and Bohemian crowd" who did him little credit, so I was curious to see them. . . . I was obliged to ask myself whether his account had proceeded from anything more

15. Jones, E., *Psycho-Analysis*, J. Cape & H. Smith (1929), p. 18.
16. Jones, E., *Sigmund Freud*, Hogarth Press (1955), Vol. II, pp. 48–9.
17. Jones, E., *Free Associations*, Hogarth Press (1959), pp. 166, 167.

than simple anti-Semitism, for it is true that they were all Jews. . . . They were all practicing physicians, for the most part very sober ones. . . .' Yet Jones, a few pages further on,[18] mentions his earlier visit at the 'birth of the famous Vienna Psycho-Analytical Society' and continues: 'The reader may perhaps gather that I was not highly impressed with the assembly. It seemed an unworthy accompaniment to Freud's genius, but in the Vienna of those days, so full of prejudice against him, it was hard to secure a pupil with a reputation to lose, so he had to take what he could get.' So, after all, Jung's impressions were much the same as those of Dr. Jones. Freud himself made no bones about his opinion of his medical associates: '. . . my long-pent-up aversion for the Viennese . . .'. And, a few weeks previously: 'I no longer get any pleasure from the Viennese. I have a heavy cross to bear with the older generation, Stekel, Adler, Sadger. . . .'[19] Jung was surprised and shocked at Freud's antagonism to his Jewish colleagues—his epithet for them was *Judenbengels*—and considered Freud's distaste for them was unreasonable, pointing out that they were intelligent people. Freud's animosity was perhaps intensified because he wanted a wider basis for the new teaching.

More and more Freud came to rely on Jung and wrote to him constantly, often every week. If Jung did not reply, he would get a telegram asking what had gone wrong. Jung has kept these letters, although he never intended to publish them; they are personal, mainly about current events, and in any case of no special importance or general interest. Dr. Ernest Jones records[20] that when he was writing his biography of Freud, 'Professor Jung generously made available his extensive correspondence with Freud'. Evidently his opinion of the letters was much the same as Jung's for he made little use of them.

During the visit to America in 1909 Freud and Jung did some mutual analysis on the outward and the return journey. This was mainly confined to analyzing one another's dreams. It was during

18. Jones, E., *Free Associations*, Hogarth Press (1959) pp. 169–170
19. Jones, E., *Sigmund Freud*, Hogarth Press (1955), Vol. II, p. 78.
20. *Ibid.*, Preface.

the course of this analysis that Jung had the dream of the medieval house which is mentioned later.[21]

In New York Freud spoke to Jung of personal difficulties—Jung did not talk of these—and asked his help in clearing them up. In due course Jung asked Freud about his dreams, and these were considered with the aid of Freud's associations, for this was the established practice at the time. All went well until a dream of a rather intimate nature came up for discussion. Jung asked for further associations as parts of the dream were obscure. Freud was quiet for a time and then said: 'No. I can't give you any further associations, for if I did I might lose my authority.' Jung mentioned this event to me more than once, and clearly it made a lasting impression on him: 'At that moment', he said, 'Freud did lose his authority.'

Thus came about the first stage in the break with Freud.[22] That Freud should wish to retain his authority had not occurred to Jung, so his refusal to give further associations came as a shock, a disappointment. Had Freud responded frankly, he would have retained Jung's respect—and also the authority which was accorded to him spontaneously by the younger man. It was at this point that Jung remarked to Freud: 'Analysis is excellent, except for the analyst.'

Jung's impatience of artificial, doctrinaire restrictions on the spread of knowledge led him in the first instance to seek collaboration with Freud, and, ironically, it was what Jung regarded as Freud's self-imposed restrictions which led to their separation.

Rightly or wrongly, Jung considered that from then onwards Freud became somewhat vindictive towards him. The precise nature of Freud's opposition was not clear just then, yet there had been a change of attitude. Jung had the clear impression that Freud could not accept the fact that he had exposed what he regarded as his weakness. There had been forerunners of this chilly atmosphere. For example, when their boat was approaching New York with its famous sky-line, Jung saw Freud gazing—as he thought—at the view and spoke to him. He was surprised when Freud said, 'Won't

21. See p. 88.
22. See p. 54.

they get a surprise when they hear what we have to say to them'—referring to the coming lectures. 'How ambitious you are!' exclaimed Jung. 'Me?' said Freud. 'I'm the most humble of men, and the only man who isn't ambitious.' Jung replied: 'That's a big thing—to be the only one.' Such episodes became important in retrospect, but even then they showed a difference in outlook, although it was not clearly formulated.

After the visit to America, Freud and Jung seldom met socially. Cordiality no longer prevailed. When Dr. and Mrs. Jung went to Vienna in 1907, they stayed a couple of weeks as welcome guests. So it was on other visits which Jung paid to Freud, and when Freud stayed with the Jungs in Küsnacht—in the house in which Jung still lives. Now the atmosphere had changed, a touch of the east wind had become evident and, although they met at conferences and Jung visited Vienna, these were formal occasions. There had been differences of opinion earlier, and too little plain speaking on both sides. But Jung appreciated Freud, although he might differ from him and criticize him: this is the ordinary, healthy relationship of colleagues. There was never any master-pupil relation between them, such as obtained between some members of the Viennese group and Freud, and this did not make Jung any more popular with them.

On one occasion Jung questioned Freud about his eleven cases of hysteria, all of whom, it was believed, had suffered sexual trauma as children. At that time Freud thought the trauma had caused the hysteria. 'But,' Jung said, 'hysterics make up these things; they want to interest you. They find out what interests you and then invent the trauma, and you believe it. But the important thing is whether the incident is true or not.' Freud thought there might be something in this and told him he had once treated a girl, the daughter of a friend. He could find no evidence of sexual trauma in childhood, but he persisted, and finally the girl invented a sexual trauma of rape by her father at the age of four. Freud said the incident could not be true, because he knew the girl's father: he was his friend, and such a thing could never have happened. So he concluded that the girl had made it up. 'But,' said Jung, 'what of the other cases? Did you know the fathers of these patients? If they had been your friends it might have turned out that these stories weren't true either, but had been invented by the patients to fit your theory.' Freud, he added, was terribly keen on these theories; nothing must interfere with them, and if anything did he would not listen. He must have a dogma, and it must not be touched. 'I have no dogma', said Jung, 'no fixed theory which must not be upset. If anyone has a better theory than my concept of the anima, for instance, then I will accept it, for I am interested only in facts, not in theories.'

Freud explained religious experience as an illusion because he seemed unable to understand it. It astonished Jung that Freud could think in such a simple way of a range of experiences which had been of value to generations of reasonable people of every age and race. If this was an illusion, it had a remarkable capacity for survival. Freud, it seemed, must explain everything rationally—a process well described in the term Ernest Jones devised years later, 'rationalization'. Even at their first meeting, spirituality was dismissed by Freud as nothing but sexuality in an altered form. Such an undervaluation was typical of his approach: everything must be reduced to something else. At one time Freud's theories seemed to point to a unitary concept of mental energy, and Jones tells us that his theory of narcissism, first mentioned in 1914, after the break with Jung, enabled him to avoid the danger of having to recognize a monistic view of life.[23]

Jung himself had not a little experience of this Freudian undervaluation. After his separation from Freud, Jung had what he considered clear indications that Freud had put about the notion that he (Jung) was a bit odd in his outlook. This naturally came as a shock to Jung, for he trusted Freud implicitly at one time, opened his mind to him and held nothing back. Some of his ideas, no doubt, seemed strange to Freud. For Jung the direct approach, the direct method of expression, had the main appeal; any beating about the bush irritated him, and still does. There was nothing cautious, circumspect or worldly-wise about his conversation or his letters to friends. And in those days he regarded Freud as a friend.

23. Jones, E., *Sigmund Freud*, Hogarth Press (1957), Vol. III, p. 294.

Freud and Jung had many discussions on the psychoanalytical theory of libido. Freud himself refers to these discussions, it appears, when he writes: '. . . it seemed for a time inevitable that libido should become synonymous with instinctual energy in general, as C. G. Jung had previously advocated.'[24] Jung often tried to convince Freud that libido could not be only one thing; that it must have some opposite. But Freud would not agree. Jung mentioned a brilliant woman, Sabina Spielrein, formerly a pupil of his, though later associated with the psychoanalytical movement, who got a Chair at the University in St. Petersburg. She wrote a paper on Jung's theory of the split libido for the *Fahrbuch*. From this paper, so Jung held, Freud derived the idea of life and death instincts in opposition, 'this hypothetical death instinct'[25] in antithesis to the instinct preserving organic substance. Dr. Jones frankly points out[26] that these new theories received a very mixed reception among the followers of Freud, as well as devastating criticism from biologists.

Jung recalled that on Freud's fiftieth birthday, in 1906, his associates in Vienna had a large medal made by the sculptor Schwerdtner, bearing on the front the face of Freud and on the reverse Oedipus solving the enigma of the Sphinx. This was presented to Freud, and at the function he became pale and agitated, though he did not faint.[27] Although Jung did not meet Freud till 1907, he was given one of these finely executed medals. The so-called riddle of the Sphinx Jung described as a sort of nursery story. It occurs in various forms: What is four-footed, two-footed, three-footed? Or What walks on four legs in the morning, two in the afternoon, and three in the evening? This is of course, the crawling baby, the adult walking upright, and the old man with his stick.

The Oedipus complex, so Jung thought, was Freud's own complex—was typical of him; his tendency was to undervalue: things were not what they seemed to be but were always something else.

24. Freud, S., *Civilization and Its Discontents*, Hogarth Press (1930), p. 96.
25. *Ibid.*, p. 97.
26. Jones, E., *Sigmund Freud*, Hogarth Press (1957), Vol. III, pp. 296–300.
27. Jones, E., *Sigmund Freud*, Hogarth Press (1955), Vol. II, p. 15.

He was constantly looking for what lay behind the scenes; how to bring things down. Freudian psychology is neurotic psychology because it is based on patients, and patients are always pleased if someone has a theory which explains their trouble. In the treatment of somatic disease no one would think of confining attention to the cause, for the disability must be dealt with in the present. So, with psychological disorders, it is a limitation always to search for causes—for example, to blame matters on the parents: Why not have the parents as patients?

As an instance of this tendency to depreciate, to look for a secondary meaning, Jung mentioned an episode at Bremen where he, Freud and others met on their way to the United States. Before coming Jung had read of the discovery in the neighbourhood of Bremen of the remains of long-dead Moors. These remains were centuries old; the bones had been dissolved by the acids in the humus, but the skin was intact. His curiosity was aroused, and after considerable enquiry in the hotel and elsewhere, he learnt that the corpses were in Schleswig-Holstein. He knew also of completely preserved bodies of Teutons in the *Bleikeller*, or lead vault, of the twelfth-century Cathedral of St. Peter in Bremen. These were matters of historical and even anthropological importance and he was determined to see them. To Jung's surprise Freud got very irritated by this keenness to see the dead bodies, and jumped to the conclusion that his concern about them indicated a wish for his (Freud's) death.[28] Jung looked on this as quite fantastic, for he was incapable of thinking in such a tortuous fashion. 'I had branded myself', he said, 'in becoming identified with Freud. Why should I want him to die? I had come to learn. He was not standing in my way: he was in Vienna, I was in Zürich. Freud identified himself with his theory—in this case, his theory of the old man of the tribe whose death every young man must want; the son must want to displace the father. But Freud wasn't my father!'

At lunch there was a discussion about the dead bodies, and Freud became very upset and fainted.

28. See p. 89.

This was the first time Freud fainted during Jung's acquaintance with him; he had a second attack during the Munich conference in 1912, and there can be no doubt about the emotional atmosphere on that occasion. At lunch there was an argument concerning the Egyptian King Amenhotep IV. Freud remarked that this King had defaced the monument erected in honour of his father, and gave this as an illustration of a son displacing the father. Such an act could only mean resistance to the father; but Jung could not accept what he knew to be a misunderstanding, on Freud's part, of the son's act. He pointed out that there was nothing unusual in those days for a son to deface his father's monument; many of the Pharaohs had done the same thing in order to have a monument for their own use, just as they emptied tombs to secure a tomb for themselves. Jung had been particularly interested in Amenhotep IV and described him as a most original and progressive thinker and as the 'father' of monotheism. There could be no question of Amenhotep's action being explained as a father complex. Freud was very much upset at being corrected, and at once went on to criticize Jung and Riklin—a colleague of Jung's—for writing articles about psychoanalysis without mentioning his name. Suddenly he fell down in a faint and Jung carried him in his arms to a couch in an adjoining room. Jung told me that when Freud recovered 'he looked up with an almost affectionate and grateful glance, as if I were his father or mother'. Jones, who thought Freud was taking the discussion rather personally, tells us that his first words when coming round were 'How sweet it must be to die'—in the arms of the mother, for instance—'another indication that the idea of dying had some esoteric meaning for him'.[29] The late Dr. Leonhard Seif was present at this lunch party and described it to me; his account confirmed Jung's version in every detail.

Jones gives a remarkable explanation of Freud's two fainting attacks: The conversation, he maintains, concerned 'the fanatical anti-alcoholic tradition of Burghölzli[30] [Forel, Bleuler, etc.], and

29. Jones, E., *Sigmund Freud*, Hogarth Press (1953), Vol. I, p. 348.
30. See p. 39.

Freud did his best to laugh him [Jung] out of it'. Jones—he was not at Bremen—then records that Freud fainted at Bremen in 1909 and again at Munich in 1912, after he 'had won a little victory over Jung'.[31] The 'little victory' refers to Freud's attempts to laugh Jung out of his adherence to the hospital rule at Burghölzli that the staff must be total abstainers. That his own jocularity, at Jung's expense, caused Freud to faint on two occasions is indeed an unexpected sequence of events!

Dr. Jones read a paper before the Medical Section of the British Psychological Society, and I was one of his audience. At a certain point in his discourse a woman fainted and was carried out. When the commotion was over, Jones, with a smile, remarked, 'Well, we can all guess why she fainted just then!' One can imagine Jones's retort had someone disagreed, saying the woman had fainted because she had made a joke at her neighbour's expense!

Early in 1910 the second Psychoanalytical Congress was held at Nuremberg, and there the International Psychoanalytical Association was founded. Jung was to be perpetual President, with absolute power to appoint and depose analysts. Wittels, in his biography of Freud,[32] gives a glimpse behind the scenes and records that the Viennese supporters of Freud, particularly Adler and Stekel, were utterly dismayed by the proposals, which meant that the scientific writings by members of the Association must be submitted to Jung for approval before publication. In addition, responsibility for the further development of psychoanalysis was to be taken out of the hands of Freud, the founder, and entrusted to Jung. Such plans must be resisted. It may be interposed that these were not Jung's plans. 'On the afternoon of this memorable day', Wittels continues, 'the Viennese analysts had a private meeting in the Grand Hotel at Nuremburg to discuss the outrageous situation. Of a sudden, Freud, who had not been invited to attend, put in an appearance. Never before had I seen him so greatly excited. He said: "Most of you are Jews, and therefore you are incompetent to win friends for the new

31. Jones, E., *Sigmund Freud*, Hogarth Press (1955), Vol. II, p. 165.
32. Wittels, F., *Sigmund Freud*, George Allen and Unwin (1934), p. 140.

teaching. Jews must be content with the modest rôle of preparing the ground. It is absolutely essential that I should form ties in the world of general science. I am getting on in years, and am weary of being perpetually attacked. We are all in danger." Seizing his coat by the lapels, he said: "They won't even leave me a coat on my back. The Swiss will save us—will save me, and all of you as well."'

Wittels resigned from the Psycho-Analytical Society in 1910 and threw in his lot with Stekel. He sent a copy of the biography to Freud in 1923 and received his permission to print his letter of acknowledgment. Freud was quite frank with Wittels: 'You know too little of the object of study, and you have not been able to avoid the danger of straining the facts a little in your analytical endeavors.'[33]

While Jung's friendship with Freud started harmoniously, it never moved altogether smoothly. Freud could be brusque and impatient if anything was suggested in discussion which he did not quite understand, and this may well have meant that he wanted time to think over what had been said. But if so his intention was not clear, and his colleagues were hurt or irritated. On one occasion the term 'introversion' (coined by Jung) cropped up in discussion. Freud brushed it aside with the casual remark, 'That is only narcissism.' 'Excuse me, Professor', said Jung, using the formal address he employed with Freud, 'introversion is not narcissism and has nothing to do with it. It is a term I introduced to describe something entirely different.' Freud made no reply. Such pin-pricks puzzled Jung who had no desire to score at Freud's expense. In spite of these minor irritations, Jung was still much impressed by Freud, although he was constantly aware of the constraint due to his need to have a complete system, an authoritative body of knowledge. Again and again Freud insisted that a dogma was an essential safeguard to prevent the black cloud or black flood of occultism from swamping his original work, which, quite rightly, he valued highly. By this Freud sometimes meant religious ideas, but more usually the phrase referred to the unconscious which, in itself, apart from the personal

33. Wittels, F., *Sigmund Freud*, George Allen and Unwin (1934), p. 12.

circumstances of the individual, had no meaning for Freud, and so he was disposed to depreciate, to defeat, or to overcome it and take it, so to speak, on his own terms.

Jung looked on the mind, and particularly the unknown, unconscious parts of it, as something to be explored, a natural phenomenon about which there was much to discover. How could we possibly say that it must be so and so? Was there any reason to conclude that the hidden background of the mind was less complicated, of simpler structure, than the conscious aspects of which we did know something? But Freud held to his conviction that knowledge must advance only along certain lines. As time went on his early discoveries—at the time a surprise to Freud—gradually came to be regarded as established, settled teaching, foundations on which the edifice was to rise. At all events, this was how it seemed to Jung. Ernest Jones (with special reference to Freud) mentions the peculiar difficulties of pioneers in steering a course between open-mindedness and degeneration into dogmatic beliefs. Freud was 'quite immune to opposition or criticism from other people, but he remained always open to the pressure of new facts. . . . They had, however, to be facts he himself observed; he did not easily take into account facts observed by other people, even by his co-workers and friends. . . . So long as he was the main discoverer in the new field, and this was in fact so during most of his life, his attitude was successful, but plainly it could not permanently stay so when other explorers appeared. In that event there would be the danger, sooner or later, of the hardening into dogmatism which in fact he just avoided.'[34]

Evidently dogmatism was something to beware of, and yet Jones himself fell a victim to it. As early as 1929 the Oedipus complex is described as 'the most characteristic and important finding in all psycho-analysis. . . . All other conclusions of psycho-analytical theory are grouped around this complex, and by the truth of this finding psycho-analysis stands or falls.'[35]

34. Jones, E., *Free Associations*, Hogarth Press (1959), p. 203.
35. Jones, E., *Psycho-analysis*, Benn (1929), p. 36.

Jones's dogmatic statement amounts to saying that the Oedipus complex is absolute truth. Jung's position in this matter is unequivocal: he regards the Oedipus complex as an assumption, justifiable in certain instances; but to universalize its application would be fantastic. What about women? It could never apply to them. Jung suggested the term 'Electra complex' to Freud, but he was not attracted to this concept.

It may be questioned whether Jones is correct in stating that Freud just avoided 'hardening into dogmatism'. Dalbiez,[36] writing on the General Theory of the Neuroses, observes: 'Freud . . . takes no care to distinguish his method from his doctrine. He regards his work as forming a solid whole. He is particularly devoted to his sexualist interpretation of transference, for it is bound up with his aetiological theory of the psychoneuroses.' This is how Jones, the most considerable of Freud's disciples, sums up his master's ideas on the origin of the psychoneuroses:

'Increased knowledge in aetiology means an increased precision in estimating the relative significance of the various pathogenic factors. In place of an ill-defined group of banal causes, we come to distinguish a specific cause for each disease, and, by the side of this, various predisposing and exciting factors. For instance, whereas thirty years ago general paralysis was thought to be due to the combined action of a variety of agents, such as heredity, mental strain, alcoholism, and so on, it is now known invariably to result from a specific cause—namely, syphilis—the other factors playing a relatively subordinate part in its production. In the past fifteen years, thanks to the researches of Freud, we have learnt to recognize the specific cause of the neuroses—namely, some disturbance of the sexual function; in other words, one maintains that no neurosis can possibly arise with a normal sexual life.'[37]

From such statements it should be clear that Jung was not emo-

36. Dalbiez, R., *Psychoanalytical Method and the Doctrine of Freud*, Longmans Green (1941), Vol. I, pp. 216–17.
37. Jones, E., *Papers on Psychoanalysis*, Baillière, Tindall and Cox (1950), p. 384.

tionally biased or mistaken in judgment in his remarks about Freud's proneness to dogmatism.

Jung never thought Freud always dogmatic, always assertive, about every subject. Had it been so, collaboration would not have been possible; but it did become more and more difficult as time went on. Jung criticized Freud's methods, his unyielding attitude, and, as he thought, the tendency to close his eyes to material which conflicted with his own theory. Freud laid unusual emphasis upon any subject he had thought deeply about, as though the mere fact that he had thought it out established its validity. This surprised Jung very much, and it was only after long acquaintance that it dawned on him that Freud's mind worked in this way and that his dogmatism was inevitable. It was not that Freud had no feelings—of course he had. Jung himself told me that Freud had a pleasant, even kindly, manner with patients, and it is certain that this contributed very much to his successful treatment. But in his teaching such characteristics find little place. His feelings were in the background, as though they were of no importance and had nothing to do with his scientific contributions. Freud himself states that he took measures to destroy all traces of his personal life—especially details of his early life: diaries, letters, scientific notes—'All my thoughts and feelings about the world in general, and in particular how it concerned me'—were done away with. It gave him pleasure to picture the discomfiture of his biographers.[38] One may suppose that the record of the self-analysis, which Jones[39] regards as a unique achievement, disappeared with the rest. Wittels's decision to write a biography of Freud came as an unwelcome surprise: How could that be of interest to anyone? His contributions to knowledge, so carefully thoughtout, surely these alone mattered. In thanking Dr. Wittels for sending the book, Freud writes: 'I need hardly say that I neither expected nor desired the publication of such a book. It seems to me that the public has no concern with my personality, and can learn nothing from an account of it. . . .'[40]

38. Jones, E., *Sigmund Freud*, Hogarth Press (1953), Vol. I, Preface.
39. *Ibid.*, p. 351.
40. Wittels, F., *Sigmund Freud*, George Allen and Unwin (1924), pp. 11–12.

On the face of it, that is a surprising assertion! Freud's personality would surely be of interest to anyone concerned with his work. But he was not disposed to satisfy curiosity on the matter; he considered his judgments on the devious working of the mind, especially in relation to other people and to circumstances, were of much greater value; object relationships were more significant than a recital of personal and private matters.

Freud and Jung worked together for six to seven years, and their separation has been the subject of interminable speculation. Feelings have run high amongst their pupils. Many of Freud's followers—who were more vocal than Jung's—seemed unable to find anything good to say about Jung, a poor compliment, by the way, to Freud's capacity as a judge of character. Jung himself often criticized Freud, but he never underrated his great qualities. Dalbiez's opinion on this is relevant: 'Bleuler and Jung diverged from Freud, and each proceeded to work out his personal views in a different way. Yet they deserve a tribute for their loyalty, in that they never fail to recall, in the works which they published after their rupture with Freud, all that they owe to him.'[41]

Making allowance for exaggeration and hasty words, it is clear that the break between Freud and Jung had been a possibility for years before the final parting. Even at their first meeting they did not see eye to eye,[42] and there had been many sharp differences in the few subsequent years. Jung was always punctilious in giving credit to Freud, but all along he was aware of differences: 'Freud has not penetrated into that deeper layer of what is common to all humanity. He ought not to have done it, nor could he do it without being untrue to his cultural historical task. And this task he has fulfilled—a task enough to fill a whole life's work, and fully deserving the fame it has won.'[43] 'The contrast between Freud and myself goes back to essential differences in our basic assumptions. Assumptions

41. Dalbiez, R., *Psychoanalytical Method and the Doctrine of Freud*, Longmans Green (1941), Vol. I, p. 178.
42. See pp. 35, 36.
43. 'Sigmund Freud in His Historical Setting,' *Character and Personality* (1932), I, p. 55.

are unavoidable, and this being so, it is wrong to pretend that we have made no assumptions. That is why I have dealt with fundamental questions; with these as a starting-point, the manifold and detailed differences between Freud's views and my own can best be understood.'[44] Nevertheless, Jung was puzzled—even shocked—that Freud was unable to appreciate what, to others, seemed reasonable developments. To Jung the personal problems and complications were in themselves of no particular importance, for he was more concerned with his work than with such details. Consequently the final parting brought unwelcome disillusionment. Jung had been astonished at Freud's refusal to give his associations concerning a dream during the period of mutual analysis.[45] But this was accepted with regret; the work went on. When Jung wrote the second part of his book, *The Psychology of the Unconscious*, he thought Freud would be seriously upset and unable to accept his conclusions. His wife argued that a highly intelligent person like Freud would be bound to admit the validity of his arguments. But as it turned out Freud did not accept Jung's ideas, and regarded them as an unjustifiable extension of his psychoanalysis.

Those who could judge only by external appearances concluded that the publication of *The Psychology of the Unconscious* brought about the cleavage, for Jung had certainly gone much further than Freud. Freud was definite in saying that Jung's views were no longer acceptable. And so the paths separated. At once this raised a question in Jung's mind which was a concern to him then—and to many since—namely, how was it that two intelligent people, dealing with approximately the same group of patients, concerned with similar philosophical and academic problems, were unable to work together?

From the practical point of his career Jung had good reason to think that the separation from Freud would be disastrous. But that did not disturb him unduly. After all, he had nothing to gain and much to lose when he joined forces with Freud originally. Freud was

44. *Modern Man in Search of a Soul*, Kegan Paul, Trench, Trübner (1933), p. 142.
45. See p. 42.

not widely known in those days and his reputation was based largely on misconceptions of his writings, whereas Jung's standing as a writer and teacher was high; he was looked upon as a coming man. Soon after he threw in his lot with Freud he gave up his University appointment. No pressure was put upon him by the University authorities to resign, but he felt his presence was an embarrassment to his colleagues, and confusing for the students, because his teaching on some important matters was not generally acceptable. It should be mentioned also that when he withdrew from the psychoanalytical movement he parted company from many colleagues whom he had reason to call his friends. This may be overlooked, for those who have written most on the Freud-Jung split write as disciples of Freud and seem determined to make Jung the villain of the piece. It is obvious from the published accounts of what took place at Munich in 1913 that many regretted Jung's departure.

It was in that year that Jung's connection with the psychoanalysts ended, following a meeting of the International Association. The second part of Jung's *The Psychology of the Unconscious* came under discussion. Freud, as we have seen, declared that Jung's work and claims could not be regarded as legitimate developments of psychoanalysis.[46] Nevertheless, three-fifths of those present voted in favour of Jung's re-election as President of the International Association for another two years, and Jung actually held the post, although the outbreak of war made it impossible to hold meetings. According to Jones,[47] seventy-four votes were cast: fifty-two for Jung's re-election and twenty-two against. He also mentions Abraham's suggestion that those who disapproved of Jung's re-election as President should abstain from voting. Some did so, including Jones himself, but the number of dissidents is not given.

Jung was deeply concerned about the dispute and so was Freud. But they never met after this stormy conference. It is profitless to stir up the dust of controversy at this distance. What occupied Jung's

46. Wittels, F., *Sigmund Freud*, George Allen and Unwin (1924), p. 178.
47. Jones, E., *Sigmund Freud*, Hogarth Press (1955), Vol. II, p. 115.

mind particularly was the problem of why a break had to come. He had no desire to set up on his own in opposition to Freud. Although there had been differences of opinion before, this, while unfortunate, could not be taken as accounting for the whole matter. Obviously Freud, like Jung, was intent upon the advancement of psychological knowledge, and with it understanding of the mind in health and in sickness. Jung at once saw that personal disagreements alone, however emotionally tinged, would be insufficient to explain the split. Here surely was an important problem. Many were familiar with the circumstances; but Jung alone considered the clash as a psychological phenomenon that must be investigated. It was easy for protagonists of Freud to pour scorn on Jung, but this did not enlighten those who found it difficult to comprehend what looked like the squabbles of men who claimed to know how adjustment to life might be reached. Often enough remarks leveled at Jung did little more than proclaim the state of mind of the critics. Here was a singularly important situation, and it was rather paltry to brush aside Jung's work with a casual observation about his 'defection' or 'revolt' from Freud as though the separation came from pique or ill-will. Even Freud himself seemed to treat the issue in a disappointingly offhand manner.

With a brief allusion to 'two secessionist movements' Freud, writing in 1925, concludes: 'The criticism with which the two heretics were met was a mild one; I only insisted that both Adler and Jung should cease to describe their theories as "psycho-analysis". After a lapse of ten years it can be asserted that both of these attempts against psycho-analysis have blown over without doing any harm.'[48] Jung's critics might well drop these negative estimates when they remember that Freud and Jung parted company nearly fifty years ago and Jung's work has developed along lines which owe nothing to Freud's influence. Those who still harp on the theme of 'defection' and 'revolt' have not kept pace with the trend of Jung's thought.

Jung was not interested in attacks and counter-attacks. He had more pressing matters to think of: his aim was to understand the

48. Freud, S., *An Autobiographical Study*, Hogarth Press, (1935), pp. 96, 97.

elements and principles on which his work rested. He was surely right in seeing the clash with Freud from this point of view, for here was an outstanding example of failure in human relationship.

Jung could not possibly study his own rift with Freud objectively, so he decided to investigate a similar problem—the conflict between Freud and one of his earliest followers, Alfred Adler. This profitable bit of research threw light upon the Freud-Adler clash, and this in turn proved to be the starting point of Jung's work on typology, which bears directly on the Freud-Jung problem, a subject dealt with in the next chapter.

Freud himself came in for considerable criticism from another quarter: it was hinted that whatever is of value in psychoanalysis is merely borrowed from the ideas of Janet.[49] At a meeting of doctors in London it was asserted that Freud appropriated Janet's ideas and produced them as his own. I wrote to him and asked if I was correct in stating that this was false and that Janet's teaching had no effect on his work. His brief reference to Janet in his *Autobiographical Study*[50] was familiar, and I mentioned it in my letter. In a long reply Freud made the matter perfectly clear. He told me that the observations of Breuer, upon which he had built further, were quite independent of those of Janet, and in fact were made years earlier though they came into the open at a later date. He continues: 'Personal relations with Janet I have never had. I am older than he. When I studied with Charcot in 1885 and 1886 I never heard Janet's name, nor since then have I ever seen him or spoken to him. From the beginning Janet set himself malignantly against my psycho-analysis and has brought forward some arguments against it which I must designate as unfair.'

In June 1932 Freud was good enough to receive me at his house in Vienna, and this was my first meeting with him. I recalled our correspondence, and he knew I was not a psychoanalyst. Before I left he enquired if there was any special question I would like to put to him. I asked if he would mind telling me how he felt about a perplexing subject: Why was it that he and the other pioneers in psy-

49. Freud, S., *An Autobiographical Study*, Hogarth Press (1935), p. 54.
50. *Ibid.*

chological medicine were on such bad terms with one another? I added that I had talked to Adler and to Stekel a day or two earlier and that I knew Jung. Freud answered readily: Inevitably some people must separate themselves and work alone and this cannot be avoided and need not be objected to. Adler's departure was not a loss; Freud had no regrets at his going for he was never an analyst. Stekel he described as a very clever man, and he was an analyst. But separation from him was unavoidable because of personal characteristics in Stekel himself which made co-operation with him impossible. I then asked about the rupture with Jung. Freud, after a pause, said very quietly, 'Jung was a great loss'. No more was said.

We may perhaps speculate that if Freud and Jung had continued their collaboration the gain to psychiatry would have been enormous. Who can tell? Divisions and controversies are not without their advantages. Be this as it may, it is certainly regrettable that the differences between Freud and Jung were not limited to scientific matters but became a focus for acrimony. Jung took no part in fanning the flames, for he was quite disinterested in such matters as anyone who knows him intimately will confirm.

One subject in particular provoked a remarkable display of ill will on the part of some who apparently did not know Jung and seemed not to have read what he had written. This came to my knowledge in 1946, when I visited Jung for the first time after the war and with surprise heard from him, and from his wife, that he had been blamed for showing anti-Semitic and pro-Nazi tendencies. Having known him in the pre-war years and having heard in public and in private his views on Hitler, it was difficult to take the matter seriously. Jung, however, felt it necessary to reply, for he thought it possible that his accusers, who had not raised the matter with him personally, were unaware of the numerous references in his writings to political events in Europe from 1918 onwards. This reply was published in Switzerland, in Germany, in 1946, and any who may have lingering doubts should read it, and in particular the opening chapter, 'Wotan', one of the five essays in this small volume,[51] for it

51. *Essays on Contemporary Events*, Kegan Paul (1947).

is a reprint of a lecture given and published in 1936. No one who read it then or who reads it now, with an open mind, could think of him as pro-Nazi or anti-Semitic. Nevertheless—such is the influence of emotion—this essay has been quoted as evidence against Jung. Such misunderstanding is hardly believable. Here are Jung's words: '. . . the abysmal depth and unfathomable character of old Wotan explain more of National Socialism than all the three reasonable factors put together. There is no doubt that each of these economic, political and psychological factors explains an important aspect of the things that are happening in Germany, but Wotan explains yet more. He is particularly enlightening as to the general phenomenon which is so strange and incomprehensible to the foreigner that he cannot really understand it however deeply he may consider it.'[52]

That he could be thought to have leanings towards Nazism struck Jung as having an element of the ridiculous, for he knew from a reliable source that his name was on the Nazi black list and that he would be one of the first people to be imprisoned, and probably shot, if the Germans invaded Switzerland. Invasion was constantly expected, for northern Switzerland was 'wide open', and while the Swiss Army was mobilized and occupying defensive positions, it was realized that effective resistance was impossible. In consequence, a *refugium* had been constructed in the Alps so that women, children and men over military age could be evacuated from the danger zone to a place of safety. Küsnacht-Zürich, near Zürich, where Jung and his family lived, was well within the danger area. Mrs. Jung's home before her marriage was in Schaffhausen, and Jung heard from relations how matters were going on that frontier of Switzerland. On one occasion he received information that a German invasion was imminent and he was strongly advised to take his wife and some members of his family to the mountain refuge. A small quantity of petrol had been kept in reserve for this purpose. At the same time he was reminded that his name was on the black list. He had good reason to take this information seriously, for in 1940 there was published a German translation of the Terry

52. *Ibid.*, p. 7.

Lectures on Psychology and Religion given at Yale University in 1937. 'The book was still in time', writes Jung, 'to reach Germany, but was soon suppressed on account of the passages just quoted, and I myself figured on the Nazi black list. When France was invaded the Gestapo destroyed all my French publications which they were able to lay hands on.'[53] The passages quoted include the following:

'The change of character brought about by the uprush of collective forces is amazing. A gentle and reasonable being can be transformed into a maniac or a savage beast. One is always inclined to lay the blame on external circumstances, but nothing could explode in us if it had not been there. As a matter of fact, we are constantly living on the edge of a volcano, and there is, so far as we know, no way of protecting ourselves from a possible outburst that will destroy everybody within reach. It is certainly a good thing to preach reason and common sense, but what if you have a lunatic asylum for an audience or a crowd in a collective frenzy? There is not much difference between them because the madman and the mob are both moved by impersonal, overwhelming forces. . . .[54]

'Now we behold the amazing spectacle of states taking over the age-old totalitarian claims of theocracy, which are inevitably accompanied by suppression of free opinion. Once more we see people cutting each other's throats in support of childish theories of how to create paradise on earth. It is not very difficult to see that the powers of the underworld—not to say of hell—which in former times were more or less successfully chained up in a gigantic spiritual edifice where they could be of some use, are now creating, or trying to create, a State slavery and a State prison devoid of any mental or spiritual charm. There are not a few people nowadays who are convinced that mere human reason is not entirely up to the enormous task of putting a lid on the volcano.'[55]

53. *Essays on Contemporary Events*, Kegan Paul (1947), p. 78.
54. *Psychology and Religion: West and East* (1958), C. W., Vol. II, p. 15.
55. *Ibid.*, p. 47.

Apparently the Gestapo were not impressed by the rumours of Jung's alleged Nazi sympathies!

Mr. Gerald Sykes, in reviewing Jung's *Psychology and Alchemy*, made a wide survey of his contributions to psychological thought, and this included a reference to *Essays on Contemporary Events*: '. . . there is no keener analysis of Nazism than that in his [Jung's] *Essays on Contemporary Events*, which, written when Hitler's star was rising, also demonstrates the absurdity of the charges of reaction irresponsibly brought against Jung.'[56]

In 1937 Jung lectured in London on 'Psychology and National Problems', and I heard the lecture. Here is an extract from the lecture transcribed by myself at the time:

'As Christianity has a cross in order to symbolize its essential teaching, so has National Socialism a swastika, a symbol as old and widespread as the cross; and as it was a star over Bethlehem that announced the incarnation of God, so Russia has a red star, and instead of the dove and the lamb, a sickle and hammer, and instead of the Sacred Body a place of pilgrimage with the mummy of the first witness. . . . It is again Germany that gives us some notion of the underlying archetypal symbolism brought up by the eruption of the collective unconscious. Hitler's picture had been erected upon Christian altars. There are people who confess upon their tombstones that they died in peace since their eyes have beheld not the Lord, but the Führer. . . . The movement can only be compared with the archetypal material exhibited by a case of paranoid schizophrenia.'

Jung's so-called leanings towards the Nazis had as little foundation as the rumours of his anti-Semitism. An ironic element in connection with such discreditable gossip is the indubitable fact that Jung had used every means in his power to give help and support to Jewish psychiatrists and psychologists who had fled from Germany because of persecution. Many of these refugees came to London and, in common with other non-Jewish doctors, I received letters from Jung (which I still have) commending former Jewish pupils

56. Sykes, Gerald, *The New York Times* book reviews, 2nd August 1953.

and asking that they should be given friendship and professional support. In addition to giving professional and social introductions this meant in some instances acting as surety to the authorities for the political respectability of the refugees. So far as Jung knew, only one of his pupils, a German, became a Nazi.

An important paper with a direct bearing on the rumours about Jung's alleged anti-Semitism and pro-Nazi leanings was written by Dr. Ernest Harms in 1946.[57] He was familiar with the situation, and although not an adherent of the Jungian or Freudian School, he undertook the arduous job of testing the truth or falsity of the rumours by examining each statement made by Jung's detractors. His conclusions are based on published material, so it is possible for anyone interested to inspect the evidence for himself. In addition, the article is a well-documented historical report, tracing the development of modern analytical psychiatry and psychology.

Apart from its avowed aims, the paper provides a vivid commentary on the psychology of rumour, a subject of special interest and concern during periods of international strain, and, of course, in wartime. Hart,[58] in a study of the psychology of rumour, gave many examples indicating to what extent it is possible for testimony to be perverted by phantasy, by the complexes of the individual witness, by the influence of others and by the circumstance that 'rational' thinking is a comparatively rare phenomenon. Harms and others traced the origin of the rumours about Jung to Freud's observation in his *History of the Psychoanalytical Movement*: 'He [Jung] also seemed prepared to enter into friendly relations with me and to give up for my sake certain race prejudices which he had so far permitted himself to entertain.' No evidence in support of this statement exists in Jung's writings, according to Harms, and he considers that in making it 'Freud had revealed the Achilles' heel of his character-structure, a vulnerable spot of a dangerous nature.'[59] In other words, something other than rational thought was at work,

57. Harms, Ernest, 'Carl Gustav Jung—Defender of Freud and the Jews', *Psychiatric Quarterly* (1946), Vol. 20, p. 199.
58. Hart, Bernard, *Psychopathology*, Cambridge University Press (1929), p. 94.
59. Harms, *op. cit.*, p. 212.

and this would seem to be true of others, for, from the evidence Harms produced, 'most of the attacks upon Jung's name have come from fanatic followers of Freud'. He also claims that dogmatic and fanatical representatives of other schools have repeatedly attempted to minimize Jung's importance.[60]

In contrast to such insinuations is Jung's position in relation to Freud, anti-Semitism and Nazi tyranny. This is made plain in the report of his address at a meeting of the International Association of Psychotherapists at Bad Nauheim in 1934 on 'The Theory of Complexes', in which he paid homage to Freud, who was then the target of Nazi hatred.[61] He recalls that on the following day, the German press condemned Jung in violent language and 'carefully registered the number of times on which he had pronounced the hated name of Freud'. He continues: 'There would certainly have been no reason to expose oneself in this manner during these weeks of the most fanatical outburst of anti-Semitism if one had wished to ingratiate himself with the National Socialist régime and its leaders. . . . At this time German Nazism raged against the Jews and, among them, particularly Freud. . . . Since many attempts have been made to use an alleged negative attitude of Jung towards Freud as an argument, let us quote a few sentences from Jung's address. Before a German assembly in a German town, Jung said: "Without the existence of the complexes the unconscious would be—as it was for Wundt—nothing but the residue of obscure representations. Through his investigations of these dark areas Freud became the discoverer of the psychological unconscious. . . . As a logical outcome, the first medical theory of the unconscious was the theory of repression postulated by Freud, which was based upon purely empirical presuppositions, without taking into account the philosophical works concerning the unconscious by Leibniz, Kant, Schelling and Carus, up to Eduard von Hartmann."'

That there is some reason to answer these foolish attempts to belittle Jung and his work will be accepted when we note that they

60. *Ibid.*, p. 199.
61. *Ibid.*, pp. 203, 222.

still crop up. In May 1958 *The New Statesman* printed a letter headed 'Jung and the Jews'. It was clear that some still give the old rumours credence. Dr. Gerhard Adler, one of Jung's oldest pupils, himself a Jewish refugee from Nazi Germany, rejoined with a factual repudiation and rightly described the attack as due to 'utter ignorance, or worse, slander'. Sir Herbert Read, in the last letter of this correspondence, while agreeing that Dr. Adler 'has rebutted these charges at the documentary level', concludes: 'Jung, in his serene old age, can afford to ignore his detractors, and surely your readers will dismiss, with the pity they deserve, the little men who pipe their envy of the great man's fame.'

After the war Mr. Winston Churchill, as he then was, paid an official visit to Zürich and received a tremendous welcome. In the evening there was a Government reception and a banquet. Jung received an invitation and had the honour of being placed beside Churchhill. We should be right in judging from this that the base rumours circulated about him had made no impression whatever on those in a position to know what manner of man he was.

CHAPTER FIVE

Introverts and Extraverts

JUNG'S *Psychological Types* was published in 1920, and in a Foreword we read that the book was the fruit of nearly twenty years' work in practical psychology. During this long period several other volumes were written, including *The Psychology of Dementia Praecox* (1906) and *Symbols of Transformation* (previously named *The Psychology of the Unconscious*) (1912). As we know the publication of this volume marked, externally, the parting of the ways with Freud. This self-imposed separation from Freud and the psychoanalytical movement—a main interest for six or seven eventful years—meant a substantial change in Jung's activity and outlook. From being, as it were, a Freudian, he had to establish his own values, to gain a new orientation, to be himself. This meant inner as well as outer insecurity, and of these the former was far and away the more significant. In addition, there was the outbreak of war in the summer of 1914 and the consequent isolation of Switzerland. Jung was called upon for military service and was in charge of camps for interned officers and other ranks of the British and Indian Armies at Château d'Oex and at Murren. After the war he received an official letter of thanks from the British Government.

Military duty was not arduous and he had time to think, and above all to come to terms with his own unconscious, during these years of intense and restless mental activity. About this time he made his first painting of a mandala, and a colour reproduction of this appears as the frontispiece of *The Archetypes and the*

Collective Unconscious,[1] with the title 'Mandala of a Modern Man'. It was a highly productive time, and much of his later work germinated during these few years when he worked alone.

We can see then that the 'practical psychology' mentioned above covers a good deal more than the research involved in writing *Psychological Types*. While this book is, and will remain, an important contribution to the psychology of consciousness, it could never have been written without the unhesitating study of the unconscious which engaged Jung's feelings and energy almost to the exclusion of other demands. Beyond doubt this period was one of special significance for all his later work, and it played its part, too, in the 'twenty years' work in practical psychology'.

Two papers from these same few years may be mentioned, for they show the inclination of his personal psychology. 'On the Importance of the Unconscious in Psychopathology' was the title of a paper read at the Annual Meeting of the British Medical Association held at Aberdeen on the eve of the 1914–18 War. Its theme is the inseparability of the conscious and the unconscious: '. . . . unconscious virtues compensate for conscious defects. . . . In normal people the principal function of the unconscious is to effect a compensation and to produce a balance. All extreme conscious tendencies are softened and toned down through a counter-impulse in the unconscious.'[2]

A second paper, 'The Transcendent Function',[3] also shows Jung's emphasis on the inner world of the unconscious. Although written in 1916, the paper was 'lost' until 1957, when it was privately printed for the Students Association, C. G. Jung-Institute, Zürich. Since then it has been published and Jung had added a new Preface. It contains the first description of a method designed to reach the unconscious contents below the threshold of consciousness—later named 'active imagination'. Given suitable opportunity, these contents may break into consciousness. That this can be dan-

1. *The Archetypes and the Collective Unconscious* (1959), C. W., Vol. 9, Part I.
2. *The Psychogenesis of Mental Disease* (1960), C. W., Vol. 3, pp. 205–6.
3. *The Structure and Dynamics of the Psyche* (1960), C. W., Vol. 8, p. 67.

gerous is now well known: the subliminal elements, appearing in consciousness, may prove to be stronger than the conscious direction and may take control of the personality and so precipitate a psychotic episode. In 1916 the method itself and its dangers were unknown. We may be sure that Jung was speaking from his clinical experience in describing its dangers—and possibilities.

These reflections are a necessary preliminary worth consideration before we can hope to understand Jung's typology. There are good reasons for mentioning them at length, for Jung has been described as a 'conscious psychologist'—that is, one who is not much concerned with the unconscious, presumably because he attaches considerable importance to consciousness and its functions. Nothing could be further from the truth, and to insist on this odd notion borders on the ridiculous. It is no surprise to find that Jung has been criticized for the opposite point of view—namely, that he depreciates consciousness through an over-valuation of the unconscious.[4]

Jung's typology should be considered in conjunction with his whole system of thought. In other words, his description of attitude types is incomprehensible without an understanding of his views on the phenomena of the unconscious, personal and collective.

In 1912 the essay 'New Paths in Psychology' appeared, and this formed the basis of the first part of *Two Essays on Analytical Psychology*,[5] a much-revised volume which is now printed in its latest form in the *Collected Works*. Those interested in the historical development of Jung's thought will find the original versions of this essay and of the second essay, 'The Structure of the Unconscious', as an Appendix to the recent English edition of the *Two Essays on Analytical Psychology*. It is worth noting that these essays, in their original form, give the earliest statement on the theory of the collective psyche, the notion of 'pairs of opposites' and of psychological types.[6]

4. Philp, H. L., *Jung and the Problem of Evil*, Barrie and Rockliff (1958), p. 10.
5. C. W., Vol. 7.
6. *Ibid.*, pp. 269 *et seq.*

Chapters I–IV provide a comparative study of the approaches of Freud and Adler. A clinical problem is discussed,[7] first from the standpoint of psychoanalysis (Freud), and next the same problem is considered from what is called 'The other point of view: The Will to Power' (Adler). With Freud everything follows from antecedent circumstances according to a rigorous causality; with Adler everything is a teleological 'arrangement'.

'Which of the two points of view is right? . . . One cannot lay the two explanations side by side, for they contradict each other absolutely. In the one, the chief and decisive factor is Eros and its destiny; in the other, it is the power of the ego. In the first case, the ego is merely a sort of appendage to Eros; in the second, love is just a means to the end, which is ascendancy . . . if we examine the two theories without prejudice, we cannot deny that both contain significant truths, and, contradictory as these are, they should not be regarded as mutually exclusive. The Freudian theory is attractively simple, so much so that it almost pains one if anybody drives in the wedge of a contrary assertion. But the same is true of Adler's theory. It, too, is of illuminating simplicity and explains just as much as the Freudian theory. No wonder, then, that the adherents of both schools obstinately cling to their one-sided truths. For humanly understandable reasons they are unwilling to give up a beautiful, rounded theory in exchange for a paradox, or worse still, lose themselves in the confusion of contradictory points of view. . . . But how comes it that each investigator sees only one side, and why does each maintain that he has the only valid view? . . . This difference can hardly be anything else but a difference of temperament, a contrast between two types of human mentality, one of which finds the determining agency pre-eminently in the subject, the other in the object. . . . I have long busied myself with this question and have finally, on the basis of numerous observations and experiences, come to postulate two fundamental attitudes, namely introversion (e.g. Adler) and extraversion (e.g. Freud).'

As a framework, Jung's psychological theory of types seems to

7. C. W., Vol. 7, pp. 34 *et seq.*

offer a plain division of personalities in so far as it describes two characteristic groups of healthy human beings. But in fact the classification is by no means uncomplicated—rather the reverse: 'Although doubtless there are certain individuals in whom one can recognize the type at a glance, this is by no means always the case . . . one can never give a description of a type which absolutely applies to one individual, despite the fact that thousands might, in a certain sense, be strikingly characterized by it. . . . The individual soul is not explained by classification, yet at the same time, through the understanding of the psychological types, a way is opened to a better understanding of human psychology in general.'[8]

Jung's description is covering in broad lines the constitutional attitudes, or ways in which the person is naturally inclined to act, termed by him 'extraversion' and 'introversion'. In the former, mental energy and interest tend to flow outwards, and in the latter the direction is predominantly inwards. Freud, a representative extravert, considered individuals in terms of what was happening to them and how circumstances affected them. Whereas Adler concentrated upon the individual's response to circumstances—how, by plans and arrangements and protests—all designed, unwittingly, to deceive himself—he would be able to triumph or feel he had triumphed over unfavourable conditions.

Jung's terms, 'extraversion' and 'introversion', refer to two easily described[9] groups of ordinary, everyday persons. Neither is better or worse, more or less desirable, than the other. Few people have any difficulty in picturing extraversion as healthy; it appears to be a satisfactory state of mind, provided it is not carried too far. But a statement that introversion is healthy may require explanation, for many consider it is unhealthy, and also many find it difficult to believe that anything can come out of the mind which has not been put into it through education or experience. This belief is still widely held, even by those familiar, academically, with the theory of

8. *Contributions to Analytical Psychology*, Kegan Paul, Trench, Trübner (1928), pp. 302–3.
9. *Psychological Types*, Kegan Paul, Trench, Trübner (1953), pp. 542, 567.

instincts and innate capacities of the mind. Some would tear the old mosaic theory of the mind to pieces and at the same time question whether much could be found within the mind itself by introverted mental functioning.

A further reason why 'introversion' continues to be used inaccurately is due to the prefix 'intro' (*intro*version), for it suggests that when mental energy flows inward the interest of the introvert is confined, limited to himself. Consequently the introverted attitude is thought to be unhealthy and synonymous with introspection. Confusion about 'introversion' arose in the first instance because the term is given one meaning by Jung and another by Freud. Originally Jung introduced it cursorily in 1910 in describing the neurosis of the child Anna,[10] in whom increased phantasy was a feature. He also used 'introversion' in his commentary on some aspects of Nietzsche's work.[11] But when he found that perfectly healthy people were introverts, he gave up the original connotation. Freud did not follow him in this, and he restricted the term to pathological conditions: 'The return of the libido into phantasy is an intermediate step on the way to symptom-formation which well deserves a special designation. C. G. Jung has coined for it the very appropriate name of "introversion", but inappropriately he uses it to describe other things. . . . An introverted person is not yet neurotic, but he is in an unstable condition; the next disturbance of the shifting forces will cause symptoms to develop. . . .'[12] And in this sense 'introversion' is still often used in the literature of psychoanalysis. Freud's regret that Jung used 'introversion' in any except the pathological sense illustrates very well the important difference between Freud and Jung which was noted earlier: Freud sees the weak point: '. . . with a certain satisfaction he invariably points out the flaw in the crystal'.[13] But Jung is concerned first of all with what is healthy.

10. *The Development of Personality* (1954), C. W., Vol. 17, pp. 13, 16.
11. *Symbols of Transformation* (1956), C. W., Vol. 5, p. 292.
12. Freud, S., *Introductory Lectures on Psycho-Analysis*, George Allen and Unwin (1923), p. 313.
13. 'Sigmund Freud in His Historical Setting,' *Character and Personality* (1932), I, p. 49.

It is important to bear in mind the simplicity of Jung's description of introversion: in the introvert mental activity proceeds from the subject to the object, and so the introvert's response is governed by subjective factors. He is intensely interested in the world, but his concern is with the effect the object has upon him. This is what Jung means when he says the introvert turns from the object. In the extraverted attitude, on the other hand, energy goes from object to subject, so that without an object, an external form of attention, the individual is 'lost', hardly aware of himself. He feels, acts, thinks with the external object in mind, and wonders what it is. Introversion and extraversion can be distinguished in terms of motives: the introvert is concerned with the fact that *he* is moved; the extravert does not realize that he is moved and attributes everything to the object.

For Jung classification, the logical grouping of types, is the least important aspect of his typology. Students may be surprised to find that the 'General Description of Types' forms the last chapter of *Psychological Types*. Merely to classify would not be of interest to Jung; but it would be all-important for the extravert. Whether or not extraverts and introverts exist in reality is not for Jung the essence of the matter. His typology is a point of view, a sort of psychological 'tool-box'—that is, he applies certain criteria. Another psychiatrist may have a different criterion, one that suits him better. But Jung finds his typology helps him to understand people, because it enables him to make a refined rather than a crude judgment about them. To say So-and so is a pyknic type, for instance, conveys a general idea, and this has its value. But to Jung's mind the assessment of functional types does much more: it gives some understanding of the psychology of the individual.

Jung was well aware of the danger of intensified introversion (or intensified extraversion). Thus he thinks of neuroses and psychoses as healthy, so-called normal processes gone astray, and not as entities existing apart with a distinctive psychology. Because schizophrenia is an excessive degree of introversion, and hysteria, in some forms, displays an over-emphasis upon extraversion, this does not mean that introversion and extraversion are in themselves unhealthy. He would not deny a possibility of weakness: the natural can become unnatural, the healthy can become ill. But extraversion and introversion in their everyday manifestation indicate quite simply the direction of psychic activity as we find it in the average, the so-called normal person, whether the contents of consciousness refer to external objects or to the subject.[14] When introversion or extraversion is habitual, natural, one speaks of an introverted type and an extraverted type.

Jung recounts with amusement an episode which occurred in a Zürich tram. A passenger asked the conductor to let him know when he ought to alight to reach such-and-such a destination. 'You get off two stops further on,' said the conductor. The man was still seated when the stop was passed, reading his book, and the conductor suddenly noticed him and called out, 'You ought to have got off at the last stop. Now you will have to go on to the next one and walk back.' But again the passenger, absorbed in his book, would have passed the next stop had he not been reminded to get off. After he had gone, the conductor, with a scornful look, remarked, 'One of those introverts! His mind is turned in; he doesn't know what he has to do.' Naturally there was a laugh, for of course all the passengers thought they knew what was meant by 'introvert'.

It is not difficult to accept the fact—if we consider it—that the introvert is concerned with the inner quality of the objects and people he is thinking about. These are external in the sense that they are apart from his personality, just as external objects are to the extravert; but he, in contrast to the extravert, is not preoccupied with the outer characteristics of the object he observes; his interest is with the effect the object produces upon himself, with how it appears to him, how he sees it. To put the matter in perhaps an extreme way, we could say that in conversation or in listening to someone talking, he hears what is said as if he himself were speaking. This may be obscure to the thorough-going extravert and obvious to the introvert. Visual illustrations of this kind of introverted

14. *The Structure and Dynamics of the Psyche* (1960), C. W., Vol. 8, pp. 119, 120.

perception are sometimes found in Chinese pictures where the subject-matter is so portrayed that a spectator feels himself to be standing in the picture. The popular idea that the introvert's interest is focused only upon his own mental processes, and that he is in consequence thoroughly selfish, is mistaken. Selfishness can be as pronounced in the extravert as in the introvert. But its presence or absence is irrelevant. The introvert is concerned with thoughts and ideas, the 'internal' things in life; but 'internal' in such a context is synonymous with 'immaterial'. Kant would be typical of the introverted thinker; yet his thoughts were directed to ideas outside himself and on how they seemed to him.

Extravert and introvert have become popular conversational words—evidence of their adequacy to express something that needs to be expressed. This apparent simplicity has led to misunderstandings, for everyone assumes he knows the meaning of the terms. It has been claimed, for instance, that extraverts and introverts can be recognized by observing the amount and position of wear and tear on shoe leather. Journalists, knowing the popular interest, often supply a list of questions, with a classification of replies on a later page, thus providing an answer to the foolish question: Are you an extravert or an introvert? Jung made one or two caustic remarks on those who compiled such lists. His typology is not a series of watertight compartments, it is never an absolutely fixed matter which can be measured, for the types represent 'certain average truths'.[15]

From time immemorial there has been an urge to put human beings into groups and thus make the study of complicated material more manageable. Probably the best known—though least intelligible—division is that of the Greeks with their classification of personality type in accordance with the prominence of bodily humours (fluids), blood, black bile, yellow bile, phlegm. But Jung's typology is different from this and from others: 'my more limited field of work is not the determination of external characteristics, but the investigation and classification of the psychic data which can be

15. *Modern Man in Search of a Soul*, Kegan Paul, Trench, Trübner (1933), p. 96.

inferred from them. The first result of this work is a descriptive study of the psyche, which enables us to formulate certain theories about its structure. From the empirical application of these theories there is finally developed a conception of psychological types.'[16]

Professor A. C. Mace has kindly permitted the inclusion of some paragraphs from a speech he made in London on the occasion of Jung's eightieth birthday:

'Central to Psychology, however Psychology be conceived, is the theory of individual difference. Jung's *Psychological Types* was acclaimed as his "crowning work". Perhaps this was premature since in 1920 he had still much to say, but the work was undoubtedly of the first importance for the science of psychology as well as for literature and the arts. . . . It is instructive to relate his work to that of Francis Galton. True, indeed, there is nothing to be said for comparing giants by standing them back to back. In fact, if we learn anything at all from the theory of types, it is that differences in kind rather than differences in degree should chiefly attract our interest and attention. Galton and Jung both belong to the genius class, but each is a genius in his own distinctive way.

'Galton, as the father of psycho-metrics, was concerned with differences that lie along a measurable continuum. Jung was more interested in the differences between the continua themselves and the bipolarity of these continua. It would be an error to regard these two interests as opposed. Even though introverts and extraverts form a continuum with frequencies distributed in accordance with the normal curve, the important fact is that individuals who deviate from the mean deviate in two contrasted directions. The continuum is bipolar. And the continua themselves form a multi-dimensional system. This is recognized by all those psychometrists who like to speak of the "factors of the mind" or the dimensions of personality.

'Some of the subtler and more intricate developments of Jung's theory of personality do not, it is said, command universal acceptance in scientific circles. So what? Since when has universal accept-

16. *Modern Man in Search of a Soul*, Kegan Paul, Trench, Trübner (1933), p. 89.

ance been the criterion of truth? Since when has the test of greatness been the record of a Gallup Poll? If these be the criteria, where does Aristotle stand, and where Newton?

'The greatness of a man is not a function even of the number of his disciples. It is rather a function of the number he stimulates or provokes to think. By this test, Jung's eminence is not in question. He enjoys the tribute not only of his disciples, but of those who would refute him.'

However we may classify human beings—politically, ethnologically, medically—there are sure to be gaps in the classification. Jung's idea in devising this typology was twofold. To begin with, he was concerned because he and Freud had separated and at the same time he knew that the separation was not exclusively, but only in part, for intellectual reasons. In addition was the incontrovertible fact that he was not alone in finding collaboration with Freud difficult. Already there had been several splits; Adler was not the only pupil to go his own way. Secondly, Jung had been forced by the nature of his work to observe individual differences in the constitutional endowment of patients, and treatment had to be modified with this in mind. To treat all patients in the same way would be as absurd as to treat all members of a family on the assumption that they were identical.

And these significant differences were not limited to patients. Doctors had their idiosyncrasies, their individual, distinctive ways, and this was evident in everything they did—including their treatment of patients. Dr. A and Dr. B, faced with the same sort of patient or problem, approached the task differently. Clearly Fate had not ordained that one group of patients would go to Dr. A and another to Dr. B. Apart from purely technical methods, it is impossible for one doctor to copy the work of another and at the same time retain his personal touch. And the personal touch is a *sine qua non* in the treatment of psychiatric patients: there the doctor cannot maintain the impersonal detachment often adopted by the physician or surgeon who is concerned only with his patient's body.

Doctors unaware of the differences between their own personality and those of others often attribute difficulty in dealing with their patients to the latter's obtuseness. But this will not do. Highly intelligent people are found expressing opposite points of view, as we observe when conflicting medical evidence is given in Court, where also learned counsel are at variance. Jung came to the conclusion that the explanation of these differences lay in the mental make-up of the people—doctors, lawyers, merchants, men, women, or children. What was sense for one was nonsense for another: one described his observations in a certain way; another spoke of the same thing in other terms. So also with illnesses, particularly psychiatric disorders. Intelligent workers often failed to agree about the facts [*sic*] to be observed, because each, aware of his own angle, was blind to that of others. Naturally there was agreement upon certain more or less fixed matters.

Jung has never held that his is the only true, the only possible 'type' theory. Simple formulations, such as the contrast between introversion and extraversion, as Jung points out, are unfortunately most open to doubt:

'I speak here from my own experience, for scarcely had I published the first formulations of my criteria, when I discovered to my dismay that somehow or other I had been taken in by it. Something was out of gear. I had tried to explain too much in too simple a way, as often happens in the first joy of discovery.

'What struck me now was the undeniable fact that while people may be classed as introverts or extraverts, these distinctions do not cover all the dissimilarities between the individuals in either class. So great, indeed, are these differences that I was forced to doubt whether I had observed correctly in the first place. It took nearly ten years of observation and comparison to clear up the doubt.'[17]

Such preliminary ideas led Jung to draw up his well-known scheme of functional types. Introversion is not always manifest in an identical way, for one introvert acts in one way and another differently: one will give considerable weight to thinking as a function, another will be more influenced by feeling.

17. *Modern Man in Search of a Soul*, Kegan Paul, Trench, Trübner (1933), pp. 99 *et seq.*

The four main functions which eventually emerged were thinking, feeling, sensation and intuition. 'I have been asked almost reproachfully', says Jung, 'why I speak of four functions and not of more or fewer. That there are exactly four is a matter of empirical fact. But, as the following consideration will show, a certain completeness is obtained by these four. Sensation established what is actually given (that is, given by our various senses), thinking enables us to recognize its meaning, feeling tells us its value, and finally intuition points to the possibilities, the whence and whither which lie within the immediate facts.'[18]

For each of us there is a natural, effortless manner in which the mind works, and this is known as the *superior* function. In contrast is the *inferior* function, the existence of which is unknown or inadequately known to its possessor because for the most part it operates unconsciously. 'Superior' and inferior' are quite satisfactory terms so long as it is understood that one is not better or worse than the other. 'Inferior' here means undifferentiated, not clearly marked. And herein lies its importance, for the inferior function or undifferentiated manner in which the mind works, appears in the symptoms of an illness, or is closely linked with them. 'Inferior' does not indicate weakness. It is, indeed, often the reverse, for the symptoms of a neurosis, unexpected, unwelcome and mysterious, can be more powerful than the conscious 'superior' function.

The value of Jung's typology in medical practice and in everyday life is considerable. It is interesting and valuable to be able to classify individuals, but it is more important to know how to talk to them and approach them in a way which they will understand. Doctors, like other mortals, are prone to lay down the law, to give advice. Patients expect this, and the doctor may be gratified that they turn to him as a person of sound judgment. But in addition to the wisdom of the doctor there is the wisdom of the patient. Advice in itself admirable, may be acceptable to one but declined by another, although the advisor makes the assumption that sensible people should take sound advice. But people do not always do so,

18. *Ibid.*, p. 107.

and this is because one person, with plenty of common sense, happens to be an extravert, and another, similarly equipped with common sense, is an introvert. Their constitutional endowment is such that they are affected differently by the same (or at any rate indistinguishable) circumstances. Consequently, the wise psychotherapist tries to get some notion of the type of patient he is dealing with. Should he fail to do so, his efficacy as a therapist will be sadly diminished.

For a detailed description of the general attitude types of extraverts and introverts, together with the functional types of thinking, feeling, sensation and intuition, which appear in both extraverted and introverted form, Jung's writings should be consulted.[19] A simple exposition of the typology is found in a book by a former student of the C. G. Jung-Institute, Zürich.[20] Frieda Fordham[21] has also made a concise summary of Jung's psychological types. In speaking of the functional types, Jung uses the simile of a compass: 'The four functions are somewhat like the four points of a compass; they are just as arbitrary and just as indispensable. Nothing prevents our shifting the cardinal points as many degrees as we like in one direction or another, neither are we precluded from giving them different names; this is merely a question of convention and comprehensibility. . . . I value the type theory for the objective reason that it offers a system of comparison and orientation which makes possible something which has long been lacking, a critical psychology.'[22] In other words, the type theory provides a criterion for careful judgment and observation.

Every person has a quality of both extraversion and introversion, and the relative preponderance in consciousness of the characteristics of one or the other indicates the type. But—to repeat—the

19. *Psychological Types*, Kegan Paul, Trench, Trübner (1933), Chapter X.
20. See Progoff, Ira, *Jung's Psychology and Its Social Meaning*, Routledge and Kegan Paul (1953), Chapter IV.
21. Fordham, F., *An Introduction to Jung's Psychology*, Pelican Books (1953), Chapter 2.
22. *Modern Man in Search of a Soul*, Kegan Paul, Trench, Trübner (1933), p. 108.

type is never absolutely fixed. Thus Freud, in Jung's opinion, was by nature an extraverted feeling type; later he developed his thinking, although it was inferior—that is, less differentiated than his feeling. Another example was Alfred Adler. As his fame spread it came about that an extraverted attitude overshadowed and falsified his natural introversion. He was a genial, warm-hearted man and a gifted speaker, and he came to welcome the publicity readily accorded to him at popular lectures.

A superficial change of type is often found in psychoneurotic illness when external appearances may be deceptive. Further, no one is totally, through and through, either an extravert or an introvert, for below the surface, in the unconscious, the counterpart will be found in the course of analysis as a natural complement to the conscious attitude. Awareness of this hitherto unknown element often comes as a surprise to its possessor. Probably relatives have been irritated or bored with personality characteristics of which the patient was unaware. To help the patient to understand and to accept such hitherto dissociated fragments is the chief aim in psychological treatment. That these acquisitions are part and parcel of the individual is beyond doubt, for no amount of suggestion on the part of an analyst will succeed in implanting qualities in a patient if these are contrary to his natural potentialities.

During Jung's visit to London in 1935 I asked the late Francis Aveling (then Professor of Psychology at King's College, London) to meet Jung. The conversation turned to the subject of extraversion and introversion, and Aveling expressed himself freely upon what he deemed to be the flaws in this typology. Jung in reply pointed out its practical value, particularly in clinical work, when the functional types (thinking, feeling, sensation, intuition) were taken into account in conjunction with unconscious manifestations, adding that it was foolish to think of the typology only in terms of consciousness. Aveling, who was not a medical man, was impressed by this application in treatment and said he had been thinking of the typology academically and not in relation to psychological treatment, of which he had no experience. Afterwards, when I was alone with Aveling, he burst into laughter and exclaimed that Jung must think him a complete fool. 'But why?' I asked. 'Well,' he said, 'I had quite forgotten, to this moment, that Jung introduced the terms "extraversion" and "introversion" to psychology! How remarkable that he didn't tell me! He is certainly more modest than I should have been in the circumstances.'

It would not have occurred to Jung that he was being modest! He was behaving quite naturally, for he is always open to learn, always ready to revise ideas. If an alternative is produced, he will examine it carefully and, if he finds it sound, accept it without hesitation.

CHAPTER SIX

The Mind—Personal and Impersonal

CONSCIOUSNESS

We have seen in the previous chapter that consciousness is by no means a simple concept. Two people perceiving the same object may be conscious of it in different ways. In childhood and in youth consciousness is intermittent and life goes on happily with only a limited awareness of the ego; the adult, too, is often regrettably unconscious, as though still a child.

In Jung's teaching consciousness is the recognition of a link, the relation of mental contents with the ego. Without such awareness there can be no consciousness of the object: 'Without consciousness there would, practically speaking, be no world, for the world exists as such only in so far as it is consciously reflected and consciously expressed by a psyche.'[1]

Consciousness is related to the outer world through the psychological functions (thinking, feeling, sensation, intuition), and in addition there is the simultaneous contact with the inner world, the world of the unconscious. We are subject to emotions and affects irrespective of our expectations and wishes; thus we experience the impact of the unconscious. Further, from moment to moment we receive messages from the unconscious in the act of remembering; and the immediate availability of memory becomes comprehensible if we assume the existence of the unconscious.

1. *The Undiscovered Self*, Routledge and Kegan Paul (1958), p.46.

Should the co-operation of the unconscious fail, we 'can't remember'. And if this state of affairs becomes severe we suffer a loss of memory for a part or the whole of our previous life. Through memory, the relations of psychic contents and the ego are obvious.

It will be agreed that the psyche as a whole must be envisaged if we are to understand the meaning of consciousness and the meaning, too, of ourselves as individuals in the psychic totality of conscious and unconscious. An important place must therefore be accorded to consciousness, for it is the close concern of psychology and the channel through which our observations about the unconscious are expressed. Psychological treatment has the aim of increasing the span of consciousness so that there may be control over a wider range of motives many of which, though unconscious, are operative in the symptoms of neurosis.

Textbooks on psychiatry are reserved about consciousness, although they give an account of such disturbances as depersonalization, dissociation and the loss or clouding of consciousness found in psychiatric and other illnesses. This must mean that consciousness is taken for granted, something self-evident; nevertheless there has been protracted controversy upon the subject, especially regarding its derivation.

John Locke (1632–1704), a medical man and a philosopher, propounded the idea that we come into life with minds akin to a plain sheet of wax upon which experience operates through the senses. In perception the quiescent mind merely records impressions from the external world through sight, hearing, touch, etc. This sensationalist explanation, with all its inadequacy, held sway for many years and still has an appeal because it contains a partial truth.

Jung would not agree that the origin of consciousness could be explained in terms of personal experience, and he maintains a directly opposite theory—namely, that it arises in the first place from the unconscious. It is because the child's mind is still near the unconscious that it operates intermittently—that is, it fluctuates between an awareness of his individuality and the primitive tendency to look on himself as he looks on other people, without distinguishing himself from the beings and objects of the world around.[2] Between the ages of eleven and fourteen or perhaps even later, perception of personal identity and personal continuity appears, and the youth knows that he is having an experience. This awareness is something new. Previously he had been able to recall the events of earlier years, but now he sees himself as apart from them; in other words, he is conscious of himself. An example of this from Jung's adolescence was given earlier,[3] when unexpectedly and compellingly he knew he must be himself. Such an experience, which many people have had, carries its own conviction.

When it is argued that consciousness emerges from the unconscious, this does not mean, writes Jung, 'that the source originates, that is, that the water materializes in the spot where you see the source of a river; it comes from deep down in the mountain and runs along its secret ways before it reaches daylight. When I say, "Here is the source", I only mean the spot where the water becomes visible. The water simile expresses rather aptly the nature and importance of the unconscious. Where there is no water nothing lives; where there is too much of it everything drowns.'[4]

When we bring in the concept of the unconscious we introduce a theme around which there has been perpetual controversy, and this may well continue. 'I cannot but think that the most important step forward that has occurred in psychology since I have been a student of that science is the discovery first made in 1886, that, in certain subjects at least, there is not only the consciousness of the ordinary field with its usual centre and margin, but an addition thereto in the shape of a set of memories, thoughts, and feelings which are extra-marginal and outside of the primary consciousness altogether. . . . I call this the most important step forward because, unlike the other advances which psychology has made, this discovery has revealed to us an entirely unsuspected peculiarity in the constitution of human nature. No other step forward which psychology

2. Lévy-Bruhl, L., *The 'Soul' of the Primitive*, George Allen and Unwin (1928), p. 16.
3. See p. 17.
4. Philp, H. L., *Jung and the Problem of Evil*, Barrie and Rockliff (1958), p. 13.

has made can proffer any such claim as this.'[5] James also mentioned 'unconscious cerebration'.

INDIVIDUATION

When the individual consciousness, with the ego as its focus, is brought into touch with the unconscious, what follows from this association?

Jung deals with this question in his *Two Essays on Analytical Psychology,*[6] particularly in the section 'The Relations between the Ego and the Unconscious'. His original observations have been revised again and again, for this essay was first published in 1916 and appeared in English in 1917.[7]

Jung uses the term 'individuation' to denote the process by which a person becomes a psychological 'in-dividual', that is, a separate, indivisible unity or 'whole',[8] and this development naturally involves the conscious and unconscious elements. It would be difficult to think of any more important objective in psychological treatment. Conscious and unconscious influences, seen or unseen, are active throughout life, and when one becomes aware of what is going on and takes part in the process of possible development, it is reasonable to expect that healthier progress will result than if matters are allowed to drift. Jung's concept of individuation provides a practical policy and so it can be of service in the treatment and prevention of psychiatric illness. It might be asked if people ever become fully individuated. This finds no answer; we might as well ask if anyone ever becomes perfectly healthy. But no one doubts the wisdom of seeking health.

A distinction is drawn between individuation and individual-

5. James, William, *The Varieties of Religious Experience*, Longmans Green (1904), p. 233.
6. *Two Essays on Analytical Psychology,* (1953), C. W., Vol. VII, pp. 121 *et seq.*
7. *Collected Papers on Analytical Psychology,* Baillière, Tindall and Cox (1917), Chapter XV.
8. *The Archetypes and the Collective Unconscious* (1959), C. W., Vol. 9 Part I, p. 275.

ism: the latter is self-centred and prominence is given to some supposed uniqueness in the individual; whereas 'individuation means, precisely, the better and more complete fulfilment of the collective qualities of the human being. . . . it is a process by which a man becomes the definite, unique being he in fact is. In so doing he does not become "selfish" but is merely fulfilling the peculiarity of his nature, and this . . . is vastly different from egotism or individualism'.[9]

We have, then, a simultaneous activity, an interpenetration, of conscious and unconscious; it is only when both aspects of the psyche work together that the aim, the objective, of the personality may be attained. So individuation should be thought of as a process of achievement.

Everyday experience shows plainly 'the incompatibility of the demands coming from without and from within with the ego standing between them, as between hammer and anvil. . . . However different, to all intents and purposes, these opposing forces may be, their fundamental meaning and desire is the life of the individual: they always fluctuate round this centre of balance.'[10] This is possible by reason of the compensatory self-regulation between the conscious and the unconscious. Self-regulation (homeostasis) is a recognized physiological mechanism, as when the body adapts itself to meet some internal change, or when inadequacy in one part, such as the eyes, is met by increased effectiveness in other organs.

That a similar reciprocal mechanism or functioning should be found in the mind is not surprising, for the body and the mind are interrelated; together they make a whole. When mental conflict leads to neurosis, the harmonious relation breaks down and the neurosis is very often an attempt to adjust the balance, to bring about a cure.

Individuation is not in itself a final goal, but the effect of the process makes it possible to bring about a fresh direction in life and to attain in some measure a new centre, a 'mid-point of the person-

9. *Two Essays on Analytical Psychology* (1953), C. W., Vol. 7, pp. 171–2.
10. *Ibid.*, p. 194.

ality';[11] this Jung has called the 'self'.[12] This is not accomplished by subtlety or thought or in solitary reflection, but in the activities of life, as a member of the community, for it is there that the possibility of blending the seeming contradictions of the conscious and unconscious may be achieved.

Coming to terms with the unconscious is the aim in psychological analysis, and this, with its hazards and possibilities, is for most people a comprehensible way of setting in motion the individuation process. Analysis is not a simple procedure. It involves for patient and doctor hard and often frustrating work in the investigation and understanding of personal problems, and the bearing thereon of the unconscious, if the way is to be opened for development of the personality. Other methods may be used to reach the goal, and other terms may describe them. Jung is not staking a claim, patenting a discovery, but giving an account of a process—the process of individuation—which is activated when self-regulation is efficient.

Individuation is development and growth; it is not an enduring state of tranquillity, a harbour where the anchor may be dropped: like everything else in life, it is manifest in ebb and flow; no goal is permanent and unalterable. Nevertheless, we can travel hopefully if personal enlightenment should confirm what may seem to those without such an experience an abstract, speculative claim.

This sketch of the individuation process needs filling in; otherwise, almost inevitably, the impression is conveyed that here, *par excellence*, is an instance of Jung's alleged 'mystical' and esoteric proclivities. But this would be a hasty conclusion. In setting out the stages in the change which follows when an individual develops as he is capable of developing, Jung is recording an experience mentioned over and over again in other disciplines. It is not suggested that analysis is the only way to set about the task. But it is one way. 'I would not blame my reader at all if he shakes his head dubiously at this point. . . . But it is exceedingly difficult to give any examples,

11. *Ibid.*, p. 219.
12. *Ibid.*, p. 236.

because every example has the unfortunate characteristic of being impressive and significant only to the individual concerned. . . .'[13]

But that is also the situation in other spheres of science, literature and art. Advances in understanding—whatever the subject—come through individuals, and it is worth remembering that universally accepted advances in knowledge began as an idea, a hunch, a phantasy in the mind of one man. Everyone with even a fragmentary knowledge of psychology will agree that the condition of mind designated by individuation cannot be set out as a blueprint. Human nature is infinitely variable, and concepts such as 'individuation' or the 'self' cannot be formulated once and for all. Even with one person the certainty of today may be the doubt of tomorrow. Such observations as these will be unnecessary for some; but there are those who seem to expect that the ways of the mind should be set out like a map of the Underground railway.

THE UNCONSCIOUS

In the early days the unconscious, by definition, was the mysterious hinterland of the mind to which were relegated, by repression, thoughts which clashed with the standards acceptable in consciousness. Consequently the unconscious was of the same quality as consciousness, and but for the chance of repression would have remained conscious.

Jung makes a general division of the unconscious contents. There is a '*personal* unconscious, which embraces all the acquisitions of the personal existence—hence the forgotten, the repressed, the subliminally perceived, thought and felt.'[14] Glimpses of this *alter ego* might appear in unguarded moments, and analysis set itself the task of bringing these repressed, and so unrecognized thoughts into the open. It might have been assumed that as repressions were removed the unconscious would have been emptied and that suitable training of children would prevent repression taking place.

13. *Two Essays on Analytical Psychology* (1953), C. W. , Vol. 7, p. 218.
14. *Psychological Types*, Kegan Paul, Trench, Trübner (1933), pp. 615–16.

These are reasonable expectations if we insist upon a personalized psychology. But it is a mistake to think that the contents of the unconscious are exclusively personal in nature.

However unique the individual mind may appear—especially to its owner—it has much in common with other minds. Personal differences in mind, as in body, are obvious enough, but we should hardly trouble to notice them if there were no similarities, for no one is concerned to distinguish totally dissimilar objects. But a common substratum, called by Jung the 'collective unconscious', is discernible. As a member of a community the individual is not circumscribed, nor does he lose his distinctiveness in being at the same time a repository of collective attributes, such as the instincts. He may look on these unlearned activities as his private property because he cherishes and uses them with personal satisfaction, and through them he can deal competently with certain environmental situations. Nevertheless, the instincts, so personal in their manifestation, so essential for life, are part of the constitution of everyone, and cannot be classed as personal acquisitions. No one thinks of his body as wholly personal, with unique qualities; the worldwide conformity of the human body, in spite of climatic and other differences, is accepted without demur. The same is true of the mind. Nor is violence done to the particular individual, for personal is not alternative to the collective, nor collective to the personal; there is no question of either-or. No two people—not even identical twins—have the same qualities and attributes; each shares in his distinctive way the features common to all.

During the mutual analysis which Freud and Jung pursued on their voyage to and from the United States, Jung had an arresting dream. It proved to be a turning-point in his thought, and led him to surmise that behind individual differences in mental make-up lies a common basic structure. Here is the dream:

'I was in *my* house. It was a big complicated house, vaguely like my uncle's very old house built upon the ancient city wall at Basel. I was on the first floor; it was nicely furnished, "rather like my present study," ' he added. 'The room was of the eighteenth-century type and the furniture very attractive. I noticed a fine staircase and decided that I must see what was downstairs, and so I descended to the ground floor. Here the structure and fittings seemed about the period of the sixteenth century or older. It was rather a dark room; the furniture was old and heavy, and I thought to myself, "This is very nice. I didn't know it was here. Perhaps there is a cellar beneath." And there was. It was of very ancient structure, perhaps Roman. I went down a dusty much-worn staircase and found bare walls with the plaster coming off, and behind were Roman bricks; there was a stone-flagged floor. I got an uncanny feeling going down the staircase with a lantern in my hand. I thought, "Now I am at the bottom." But then in a corner I observed a square stone with a ring in it; this I lifted, and looked down into a lower cellar, which was very dark, like a cave or possibly a tomb. Some light came in as I lifted the stone. The cellar was filled with prehistoric pottery, bones, and skulls. I was quite amazed, and as the dust settled I felt I had made a great discovery. There the dream ended and I woke up.'

Jung could make nothing of this dream—though he had some 'hunches'; but he told it to Freud. He recalled how he watched Freud turning it over in his mind, thinking about it, and he wondered what he would say. Freud, concentrating on the bones and the skulls and disregarding the rest of the dream, considered it showed that there was someone associated with him who he wanted dead, for the skulls could only mean death. Freud asked if there was anyone he would like to see dead; 'No, not at all!' he answered. But, to his surprise, Freud pressed the point, and then Jung questioned him about his insistence on the dream as a death-wish and asked if he thought the reference to skulls indicated the death of a particular person—for instance, his wife. 'Yes,' replied Freud. 'It could be that. And the most likely meaning is that you want to get rid of your wife and bury her under two cellars.' He overlooked the fact that there were several skulls, not just one.

Death was often in Freud's mind, and a few weeks earlier he had jumped to the conclusion that Jung wished him dead so that he could succeed him; but such an idea had never occurred to Jung.[15]

15. See p. 46.

Concern for only one feature in the dream and lack of interest in the remainder surprised Jung. 'Well, what do you make of the other parts?' he asked, but the reply was unproductive. An unconvincing interpretation such as this seemed not to do justice to the material, and Jung felt Freud's handling of the dream showed a tendency to make the facts fit his theory, as though the theory itself was serving some purpose. Why this emphasis on the skulls and bones? Why an inclination to depreciate, to find the weak spot? It was as though the dream must be reduced to something derogatory, so that the analyst would be in a superior position. Further, the interpretation of the dream in terms of Jung's personal life did not explain it. An impressive feature in the dream—to which Freud did not refer—was the atmosphere of expectancy. It was like an exploration: from the start there was the urge to go from stage to stage; then came the mysterious finale as he looked down the steps and saw the bones and the pieces of pottery which he knew to be ancient.

Jung reflected a great deal about the dream, and came to see the house as representing the external aspect of the personality, the side appearing to the world. Inside the house—that is, within the mind or the personality—were many layers going back to medieval times and to earlier periods. Although he was quite at a loss to explain the essential features of the dream, he felt bound to assume that it meant what it said. Certainly he could get no understanding of it in purely personal terms, and an explanation in terms of possible repressed experiences seemed wholly artificial.

It occurred to him that the house might represent, as in a picture, the stages of culture, one succeeding another, just as in the excavation of ancient sites the remains of earlier buildings are revealed beneath the foundations of present-day houses. With its varied style at different levels, the house in the dream might carry some historical allusion. Could the dream have the type of structure so often revealed in human history? 'It was then, at that moment, I got the idea of the collective unconscious,' said Jung. It seemed a possible, even significant, hypothesis. The more he thought about it the clearer it became that this layer of stratum formation could be seen in the development of our own and other cultures: the old gives place to the new; the new derives from the old. Our bodies show such a development. His reflections on this dream were the origin of ideas later published in *The Psychology of the Unconscious*.

In those days his ideas about the collective unconscious were in his mind as a possibility, not yet sufficiently in focus for clear formulation, and he still thought of the conscious mind as a room above, with the unconscious as a cellar underneath. Thus the unconscious at this stage corresponded to Freud's view: its contents were entirely personal and indistinguishable from consciousness, of which it formed a part till repressed. Later, Jung's views developed and he used two self-explanatory terms, 'personal' and 'impersonal' unconscious—in other words, the psychological ego and the psychological non-ego.

To denote the impersonal unconscious turned out to be difficult, and confusion has arisen through the use of three terms, 'collective', 'autonomous' and 'objective' psyche. There is something to be said for each, and they were coined to emphasize particular aspects of the concept. So long as we know what we mean by the words we use as synonyms we can take our choice or we can use them interchangeably. But the multiplicity of terms is regrettable. 'Collective unconscious' has become familiar and is likely to survive when the others have been forgotten. Jung himself in conversation usually refers to the collective unconscious. No doubt we shall continue to find it confused with vague terms, such as 'the group mind', because of the difficulty in accepting the possibility that within the psyche there could be anything unknown, let alone anything impersonal. Time and again Jung has pointed out that his views on the collective unconscious are hypothetical, and this in itself is daunting for those who like to think of themselves as practical, down-to-earth people. Fears of the hypothetical are understandable, but not necessarily significant.

Without some assumption, observation will be diffuse and unproductive, and the stimulating quality of a provisional supposition can be immense. It is true that we may not be able to answer all the questions arising from the idea of the collective unconscious.

On the other hand, the hypothesis itself has been fruitful; it has become established, and will remain so unless advances in knowledge carry us past the stage of hypothesis.

When the concept 'unconscious' was introduced to psychology, it was received with suspicious reserve, although for centuries it had been familiar in philosophy. Leibniz, for instance, in the early days of modern philosophy, tells us that 'These unconscious [insensible] perceptions also indicate and constitute the identity of the individual . . . the *petites perceptions* which determine us on many occasions without our thinking of it. . . '.[16] Consequently, it was not surprising to find that Jung's notion of the collective unconscious was—and still is—received with disfavour and suspicion. Jung himself says: 'None of my empirical concepts has met with so much misunderstanding as the concept of the collective unconscious psyche, a functional system consisting of pre-existing forms of a universal, collective and non-personal character, which does not develop individually but is inherited.'[17]

The ways in which the collective unconscious works are called 'archetypes' (the original pattern, the prototype)—that is, an inborn manner of comprehension comparable to the instincts, which are an inborn manner of acting. Jung's teaching and reflections on the collective unconscious are explained fully in his writings,[18] and need not be summarized here.

Freud was aware of non-personal components in the mind, although he never accepted Jung's developed work on the collective unconscious. In his last major work he writes: 'Memory very often reproduces in dreams impressions from the dreamer's early childhood . . . they had become unconscious owing to repression. . . . Beyond this, dreams bring to light material which could not originate either from the dreamer's adult life or from his forgotten childhood. We are obliged to regard it as part of the *archaic heritage*

16. Leibniz, G. W., *The Monadology and Other Philosophical Writings*, Oxford, Clarendon Press (1898), pp. 373, 375.
17. 'The Concept of the Collective Unconscious', *St. Bartholomew's Hospital Journal* (1936), pp. 44, 46.
18. See *Two Essays on Analytical Psychology* (1953), C. W., Vol. 7, pp. 63, 124.

which a child brings with him into the world, before any experience of his own, as a result of the experience of his ancestors.'[19] Again: 'I believe it not impossible that we may be able to discriminate between that part of the latent mental processes which belong to the early days of the individual and that which has its roots in the infancy of the race. It seems to me, for instance, that symbolism, a mode of expression which has never been individually acquired, may claim to be regarded as a racial heritage.'[20]

In further reference to symbols: 'We get the impression that here we have to do with an ancient but obsolete mode of expression. . . . I am reminded of the phantasy of a very interesting insane patient, who had imagined a "primordial language" of which all these symbols were survivals.'[21] Then in one of his latest books Freud returns to this idea: 'The archaic heritage of mankind includes not only dispositions, but also ideational contents, memory traces of former generations.'[22] Freud's interest in anthropology was aroused by Jung: 'the explicit indications of Jung as to the far-reaching analogies between the mental products of neurotics and of primitive peoples which led me to turn my attention to that subject.'[23]

In an article[24] entitled 'Darwin and Freud', Dr. Alex Comfort says that 'Freud's idea of a primal horde in which the strongest male rules was his only obvious debt to Darwin. It was an important debt because it started him with a firmly Darwinian idea that sexual dimorphism was primarily competitive. . . . Freud did in fact recognize the Oedipal reactions as being built in. . . . Consequently he was obliged to turn to the concept of racial memory to account for something which would make sense in evolutionary terms but in virtually no others.' Comfort quotes Ernest Jones to show that Freud had some doubt about his theory of the primal horde: ' "We should

19. Freud, S., *An Outline of Psycho-Analysis*, Hogarth Press (1949), p. 28.
20. Freud, S., *Introductory Lectures on Psychoanalysis*, George Allen and Unwin (1923), p. 168.
21. *Ibid.*, p. 140.
22. Freud, S., *Moses and Monotheism*, Hogarth Press (1939), p. 159.
23. Freud, S., *An Autobiographical Study*, Hogarth Press (1949), p. 121.
24. Comfort, A., 'Darwin and Freud', *Lancet* (1960), II, p. 107.

greatly like to know", writes Freud [in 1912] "whether the Jealous Old Man of the horde in Darwin's primordial family really used to castrate the young males before the time when he was content with simply chasing them away." '[25] Freud's tentative conclusions have not been well received even by his own disciples, and anthropologists consider *Totem and Taboo* does him little credit. Dr. Howard Philp,[26] in a careful study of Freud's anthropological deductions in *Totem and Taboo* and in *Moses and Monotheism*, has demonstrated the frailty of Freud's hypotheses. Freud knew that his theories were imperfect, and, to quote Philp, '. . . even admitted it in *Moses and Monotheism*, but answered that he preferred to hold his own version. Facts of history, sound anthropology, convincing psychology in relation to the racial unconscious, evidence worthy of serious consideration or even solid argument—none of these is prominent in *Moses and Monotheism*.' We should remember, however, Freud's[27] statement that his ideas on the activities of the primal horde came to his mind as a 'hypothesis, or I would rather say, vision'.

It is true that Freud's acceptance of non-personal features in the psyche had no observable effect on his system of thought, and we can only infer that he was not interested in such things and preferred to concentrate upon the unfolding of the individual mind. He noted the impersonal facts and passed on. He uses anthropological material in support of his theory of sexual disturbances in the individual's life, although, as we have seen, his conclusions were disputed. What a contrast with Jung, who was never particularly concerned with theories, but very much with facts he had observed; who looked for evidence in support of his observations, and only accepted them when that evidence was satisfactory.

In looking back to the parting of Freud and Jung we can reflect sadly that if Freud had followed up his observations on the archaic heritage of the individual he might have found himself in agreement with Jung's conclusion about the collective unconscious. We should then have been spared the sectarianism of separate schools.

25. Jones, E., *Sigmund Freud*, Hogarth Press (1955), Vol. II, p. 502.
26. Philip, H. L., *Freud and Religious Belief*, Barrie and Rockliff (1956), p. 123.
27. Freud, S., *An Autobiographical Study*, p. 124.

An example of this is Dr. Glover's[28] fault-finding criticism of Jung and his adulatory support of Freud. And yet even he is bound to see that Freud was aware of non-personal elements in the human psyche, but these are brushed aside: 'Whether Freud's view that symbols represent phylogenetic traces is accurate or whether, as many Freudian analysts prefer to think, symbols are created in the course of individual development . . . the most convincing evidence that no approximation of concepts occurred to bridge the gulf between Freudian and Jungian systems lies in the fact that despite Freud's obvious interest in the psycho-biological aspects of the constitutional factor, *these were at all times subordinated to his concern with the unconscious aspects of individual development*. The whole structure of Freudian metapsychology is unaffected by his incursion into the region of phylogenetic speculation.' Freud's line of thought is not happily expressed by 'incursion'—that is, a hostile inroad or invasion; but Dr. Glover is insistent that, no matter what Freud may have said about phylogenetic traces, many Freudians prefer to think otherwise.

Freud's theories on racial memory and similar themes are referred to by other well-known psychoanalysts. Dr. Ernest Jones[29] disputes Freud's claim that there is evidence in support of an archaic inheritance. 'Now in the psycho-analysis of individuals we have in a number of cases been able to demonstrate that ideas closely parallel to totemistic belief had been cherished during infancy, partly consciously, partly unconsciously. . . . In other words, we have before us in the individual a whole evaluation of beliefs and customs, or rituals based on them, which is parallel to what in the field of folk-lore has run a course of perhaps thousands of years.' Thus he advances what appears to be the familiar, though not widely accepted, recapitulation theory.

Dr. Ella Sharpe,[30] having declared her acceptance of Dr. Jones's explanation of symbolism, writes: 'The chief method of distorting

28. Glover, E., *Freud or Jung*, George Allen and Unwin (1950), p. 43.
29. Jones, E., *Essays in Applied Psychoanalysis*, Hogarth Press (1953), Vol. 2, p. 7.
30. Sharpe, Ella, *Dream Analysis*, Hogarth Press (1937), pp. 53–5.

the latent content (of dreams) is accomplished by symbolism, and symbolism has to be created afresh out of individual material and stereotypy is due to the fact of the fundamental perennial interests of mankind. . . . Each individual creates symbolism afresh, such symbols as he will originate being inseparable from his environment as, for example, ships for sailors, the plough for farmers, the aeroplane and stink bombs for modern town dwellers. The truth about symbolism in this respect was once stated for me very simply years ago by a girl of fourteen who had written an essay on "Fairy Tales". She concluded it thus: "If all the fairy tales in all the world were destroyed tomorrow it would not matter, for in the heart of the child they spring eternal." ' The concluding sentence comes as a surprise, for it appears to contradict her own statement that symbols are acquired individually and to support Jung's thesis of the collective unconscious. Fairy tales, with their similarity of subject-matter and their spontaneous appearances in different countries, afford strong evidence in support of the hypothesis of the collective unconscious.

We have, then, a conflict of opinion, with Freud's recognition of both non-personal and personal features in the psyche, and, on the other hand, the refusal of certain Freudians to accept the former, insisting upon an exclusively personal psychology.

Jung, of course, accepts personal and non-personal psychic elements. His recognition of the non-personal, the collective, manifest as it is through the archetypes, is the most important and, as many think, the most fruitful concept in his entire system of thought. Of course, it is difficult to grasp such an unexpected idea! It needs some hard thinking, with observation and an open mind. Yet to understand the psyche as a whole makes the parts more intelligible. Jung's remarks on the subject are very much to the point: In a Foreword to a book[31] by one of his pupils, he writes: '. . . The concept of the archetype has given rise to the greatest misunderstandings and—if one may judge by the adverse criticisms—must be presumed to be very difficult to comprehend. . . . My critics, with but few excep-

31. Jacobi, Jolande, *Complex/Archetype/Symbol*, Routledge and Kegan Paul (1959), pp. x, xi.

tions, usually do not take the trouble to read over what I have to say on the subject, but impute to me, among other things, the opinion that the archetype is an inherited representation. Prejudices seem to be more convenient than seeking the truth.' And the prejudice may spring from conviction that scientific proof is a final court of appeal.

In May 1960 *The Archetypes and the Collective Unconscious*[32] was reviewed (by myself) in the *British Medical Journal*,[33] and in the review was this paragraph: 'Jung's hypothesis of the collective (impersonal, objective) unconscious and its mode of functioning, the archetypes, is a bold theory. Yet it is no more daring than the theory of pre-existent instincts in animals and men. The hypothesis, though lacking scientific foundation, none the less provides a more satisfactory explanation for certain psychological facts than any other at present available.' Jung wrote to me upon the question of proof and pointed out that a scientific hypothesis is never proved absolutely. His letters have a special interest, and extracts from them, and from my replies, follow:

(1) *From Professor Jung*

22nd May 1960

. . . There is only one remark I do not quite understand. Speaking of the hypothesis of archetypes, you say that there is no scientific proof of them yet. A scientific hypothesis is never proved absolutely, in so far as the possibility of an improvement is always possible. The only proof is its *applicability*. You yourself attest that the idea of the archetype explains more than any other theory, which proves its applicability. I wonder, therefore, which better proof you are envisaging. When you assume the existence of an instinct of migration you can't do better than to apply it for instance to birds, and demonstrate that there are actually birds which

32. *The Archetypes and the Collective Unconscious* (1959), C. W., Vol. 9, Part I.
33. Bennet, E. A., 'Archetype and "Aion"', *British Medical Journal* (1960), I, p. I, 484.

migrate. The archetype points that there are thought formations of a parallel or identical nature distributed all over the world (for instance, Holy Communion in Europe and *teoqualo* in ancient Mexico) and, furthermore, that it can be found in individuals, who have never heard of such parallels. I have given ample evidence of such parallels and therewith I have given evidence of the applicability of my viewpoint. Somebody has to prove now that my idea is *not* applicable and to show which other viewpoint is more applicable. I wonder now how you would proceed in providing evidence for the existence of archetypes, other than its applicability? Or can you show that the idea of 'archetype' is nonsense in itself? Please elucidate my darkness.

Reply from E. A. Bennet

27TH MAY 1960

When I say your theory of archetypes lacks scientific foundation—that is, scientific proof—this in no way lowers its value. A scientific theory can be entirely satisfactory scientifically, and at the same time untrue absolutely, because a scientific theory is concerned with possibilities and with working hypotheses. But it is not concerned with absolute truth. Of course, I know very well that you make no claim whatever about such things as absolute truth. Newton employed the scientific method, and reached conclusions which were later abandoned. But his method was quite sound. Perhaps I am wrong, but I feel that applicability of a theory would not necessarily give *scientific proof*. The importance of applicability is not in question. But scientific proof or scientific foundation would seem to claim for certain phenomena an invariable order in nature. Freud seemed to make such a claim, following the scientific outlook of the nineteenth century. Your flexibility, your empirical outlook, is far more attractive when applied, as with the archetypes, to a theory. I could not imagine that a dogma would have any attraction for you. When I said, in the review, that your theory lacked scientific foundation I felt this was one of the *virtues* of the theory . . . the strength, as it seems to me, of your method and hypothesis resides in the fact that you avoid the claim of scientific foundation or proof in the sense of claiming something absolute.

You ask what proof I am envisaging. Frankly I wasn't envisaging any proof. I agree that applicability gives the widest support for the theory of archetypes. But I don't think it gives *scientific proof*. . . .

I cannot myself see any reason to doubt the existence of archetypes. The fact of their applicability in numerous ways supports one's belief. But I would not like to think that we had got to the point when nothing more could be known of the archetypes and their manifestation. . . .

(2) *From Professor Jung*

3RD JUNE 1960

. . . There seems to be some misunderstanding in terms: by 'applicability of a theory' I don't mean its practical application in therapy, for instance, but its application as a principle of understanding and a heuristic means to an end as it is characteristic of each scientific theory.

There is no such thing as an 'absolute proof'; not even the mathematical proof is absolute inasmuch as it only concerns the *quantum* and not the *quale*, which is just as important, if not more so. I wondered therefore about your statement that scientific proof for the conception of the archetype is lacking, and I thought you had something special up your sleeve when you made it. As there is no such thing as 'absolute proof', I wondered where you draw a line between the applicability of a theory and what you call 'scientific proof'.

As far as I can see the only proof of a theoretical viewpoint is its applicability in a sense mentioned above—namely, that it gives adequate or satisfactory explanation and has a heuristic value. . . .

If this is not scientific evidence, then I must expect of you that you show me what scientific evidence would be in this case. With other words: what proof is it, in your mind, that is lacking? It cannot be an 'absolute proof', because there is no such thing. It must be what you call 'scientific proof', a special kind of proving of which you know, since you are able to state that it is lacking. . . .

I cannot be satisfied with the statement that something is lacking, because it is too vague. I know that there is always something lacking. Therefore I should be most indebted if you could tell me what is lacking, as you must have some definite idea of how such a thing should be proved otherwise than by the observation of relevant facts.

. . . It is not hair-splitting, but it has much to do with what I call 'psychical reality', a concept very often not understood. I appreciate your answer highly, since I am always eager to improve on whatever I have thought hitherto. . . .

Reply

8TH JUNE 1960

. . . you are right when you say there has been some misunderstanding about terms. You ask where I draw the line between (*a*) the applicability of a theory and (*b*) its scientific proof.

(*a*) The applicability of, for example, your theory of the archetypes as a principle of understanding has immense practical value. If applicability had not been possible, I'm sure you would have abandoned the theory long ago. As a scientific theory it gives an acceptable explanation of all known relevant phenomena, it continues to predict further phenomena and these in due course are observable. Consequently, as a scientific theory, concerned with possibilities and with a working hypothesis, it is entirely satisfactory.

(*b*) By scientific proof I mean an explanation of phenomena capable of being checked and observed by others and found to possess an unchanging and predictable order. This implies a general agreement about the nature of the phenomena—that is, the data—under consideration. Scientific proof in these terms can be found for phenomena in the non-living experimental sciences, like chemistry or physics. But my view is that it is not possible to produce such scientific proof in psychological matters. Naturally, this does not invalidate the use of a scientific theory or hypothesis.

A difficulty so far as scientific proof is concerned is in getting agreement from different workers about the data which have been observed as well as agreement on the method of observation employed. As you know, there have been differences of opinion about the phenomena you describe as archetypes. The phenomena have been explained—I think very inadequately—by the theory of recapitulation and it has been argued that this is the only sound explanation of these phenomena. Further, some Freudian analysts have argued that the archetypes are found as the personal experience of children and that Jungians are wrong in ascribing collective qualities to them. I think these analysts have misunderstood what you mean by archetypes; but that such views are held shows the difficulty in getting agreement about the data which have been observed.

When I mentioned in my review that your theory of the archetypes lacked scientific foundation or proof, I put this forward, bearing in mind the opening article in *The Times Literary Supplement* of January 29, 1960, where the author stated that 'no such archetypes as Professor Jung describes can be shown to exist'.[34] By this I understood the writer to mean that no scientific proof can be produced in support of the existence of the archetypes. This author, of course, failed to see that you were putting forward a hypothesis.

In my opinion, the absence of scientific foundation or proof is no drawback. In the present state of knowledge, the strict procedure of the non-living sciences cannot be applied to psychology. I would agree that applicability gives the strongest support and the only form of proof available in support of the hypothesis. I should not have thought it gave scientific proof which could not be disputed by anyone. I am sure you would agree that applicability alone is not proof or scientific evidence although it gives—as I said in the review—the most satisfactory explanation available for the phenomena.

I would not say . . . that the archetype itself is not evidence. I would say it was evidence, but not of the type that would be

34. See note on p. 105.

described as scientific evidence, by which I mean the type of evidence acceptable in the non-living sciences.

I hope this explanation, such as it is, is satisfactory. It does seem to me to support your statement that there has been some misunderstanding about terms. I was particularly anxious to make clear my use of the term 'scientific proof'. It is not a special kind of proving, apart from its general use in the non-living sciences. I remember very well your remarks about science in your book, *Psychology and Religion*, and I was anxious to emphasize in this review (as I have done elsewhere) that a theory could be acceptable even though it could not be proved, as proof is understood in the non-living sciences. We seem to be in a position in psychological work where there is disagreement about the data and about the methods used in obtaining and proving their reality. Consequently we cannot, as yet, secure results which could be described as laws derived deductively from the data.

(3) *From Professor Jung*

11TH JUNE 1960

. . . Thank you very much for your illuminating letter. I see from it that you understand by 'scientific evidence' something like chemical or physical proof. But what about evidence in a law court? The concept of scientific proof is hardly applicable there, and yet the court knows of evidence which suffices to cut a man's head off, which means a good deal more than the universality of a symbol. I think that there is such a thing as 'commensurability of evidence'. Obviously the way of proving a fact is not the same and cannot be the same in the different branches of knowledge. For instance the mathematical method is applicable neither in psychology nor in philosophy, and *vice versa*. The question ought to be formulated: what is physical, biological, psychological, legal and philosophic evidence? By which principle could one show that physical evidence is superior to any other evidence? Or how could anybody say that there is no psychological evidence for the existence of a quantum or a proton? Obviously no branch of knowledge can be expressed in the terms of another branch, as one cannot measure weight by kilometres or length by litres or ohms by volts. There is also no 'scientific proof' for the existence of the migration-instinct, for instance, yet nobody doubts it. It would be too much to expect chemical proof in a murder case, yet the case can be proved by a legal method quite satisfactorily. Why should psychology be measured against physics—if one is not a member of the Leningrad Academy?

Reply

17TH JUNE 1960

. . . Your line of reasoning, to my mind, is absolutely sound, and I agree entirely when you say that 'the way of proving a fact is not the same and cannot be the same in the different branches of knowledge'. I had attempted to say much the same thing—though not so clearly as you have done—in my letter of the 27th May. My statement in the review of your book, that scientific proof is still lacking for your theory of archetypes, was directed against those who make the mistake of demanding scientific proof where it cannot be applied. You would agree, I am sure, that this is often done, and those who do so frequently adopt a self-righteous attitude, as though the demand for scientific proof should always be acceptable whatever the subject under consideration. . . . It is surprising how many psychiatrists and psychologists still attach the greatest importance to scientific proof in the sense in which I used these words. This is seen in published papers and in the selection of research projects for post-graduate students. The nineteenth-century attitude towards scientific proof is still very much to the fore and it hinders research into psychological phenomena—for example, into such a subject as the phenomenology of dreams.

I appreciate your reference to the Leningrad Academy. Nevertheless, psychology—to its great loss—continues to be measured against physics, as is seen, for example, in experimental psychology, where the psyche seems to have been left out in the cold and statistics and objective measurements, despite their unsuitability, reign in its stead.

(4) From Professor Jung

23RD JUNE 1960

I can entirely subscribe to your statement: 'Its (the scientific method's) tool is the objective observation of phenomena. Then comes the classification of the phenomena and lastly the deriving of mutual relations and sequences between the observed data, thereby making it possible to predict future occurrences, which, in turn, must be tested by observation and experiment',[35] if, I must add, the experiment is possible. (You cannot experiment with geological strata, for example!)

What you state is exactly what I do and always have done. Psychical events are observable facts and can be dealt with in a 'scientific' way. Nobody has ever shown to me in how far my method has not been scientific. One was satisfied with shouting, 'Unscientific'. Under these circumstances, I do make the claim of being 'scientific', because I do exactly what you describe as 'scientific method'. I observe, I classify, I establish relations and sequences between the observed data, and I even show the possibility of prediction. If I speak of the collective unconscious, I don't assume it as a principle; I only give a name to the totality of observable facts, i.e. archetypes. I derive nothing philosophical from it, as it is merely a *nomen*.

The crux is the term 'scientific', which in the Anglo-Saxon realm means, as it seems, physical, chemical and mathematical evidence only. On the Continent, however, any kind of adequate logical and systematic approach is called 'scientific'; thus historical and comparative methods are scientific. History, mythology, anthropology, ethnology are 'sciences' as are geology, zoology, botanics, etc.

It is evident that psychology has the claim of being 'scientific',

35. Bennet, E. A., 'Methodology in Psychological Medicine', *Journal of Mental Science* (1939), LXXXVI, No. 361, p. 230.

even where it is not only concerned with (mostly inadequate) physical or physiological methods. Psyche is the mother of all our attempts to understand Nature, but in contradistinction to all others it tries to understand itself by itself, a great disadvantage in one way and an equally great prerogative in the other!

Reply

7TH JULY 1960

Your letter confirms what I mentioned before—namely, there had been some confusion of terms . . . that it was only in the sciences such as chemistry and physics that the question of proof became important. Proof being taken in these sciences to mean, in the simplest terms, that which can be demonstrated by measurement and weighing. I don't think this would apply to atomic physics—a subject with which I am not familiar, but where, I think, there is some departure from what would usually be regarded as scientific proof. In the everyday use of the term 'scientific proof' we deal with considerations wherein a conclusion is inevitable and must be accepted by everyone, provided the meaning of terms is agreed upon. I don't, of course, mean that this is absolute truth in the metaphysical sense and I agree fully with you that no one knows what 'absolute truth' means.

You mention variation in the use of the word 'scientific'. I am inclined to think that in the Anglo-Saxon realm the word, as applied to method, is used very much as it is elsewhere. On the Continent, and here as well, 'any adequate and systematic approach', to use your own words, is quite scientific. Your own approach one must certainly call scientific. . . .

NOTE

The article in *The Times Literary Supplement* mentioned in the letter of 8th June, 1960 was a review of Jung's *The Archetypes and the Collective Unconscious* and *Aion: Researches into the Phenomenology of the Self*. By way of contrast, an extract from a review[36] in *The Times Literary Supplement* of 30th December, 1960 may be given:

'Equally invisible is the power which creates not only behaviour patterns that we observe in human actions but also the images of the wise old man, the *puer aeternus*, the animus/anima and others which appear in dreams and fairy tales, and to which we give the name of archetypal images. Dr. Jacobi's lucid presentation of Jungian ideas makes a responsive reader aware of the wisdom that exists in the archetypal life of the collective unconscious.'

36. Jacobi, Jolande, *The Complex/Archetype/Symbol in the Psychology of C. G. Jung*, translated by Ralph Mannheim, Vol. 7, Routledge and Kegan Paul (1959).

CHAPTER SEVEN

Mental Life as a Process

OVER the last hundred years the evolutionary outlook which accompanied the birth of the *Origin of Species* has given a fresh stimulus to psychology. Until the eighteen-fifties psychology was subordinate to philosophy; since then it has expanded into a separate branch of study and we have seen its influence in almost every branch of life: education, industry, journalism, politics and of course medical science have all benefited from this expansion. Within the last twenty-five years the training of medical students—at any rate in these islands—has broadened to include lecture-demonstrations in the recognition and treatment of mental illness of every type.

Behind these changes lies an altered outlook arising from the acceptance of two important characteristics of modern psychology: Firstly, the mind itself is a creative entity; from birth it is capable of action, dynamic, and this has largely replaced the idea of the mind as a mosaic-like structure formed in response to experience. Second is the claim that the mind operates on the unconscious as well as on the conscious level. These propositions, so commonplace in our time, were distinctive features in the youthful psychology of the late nineteenth century. When Jung began his career at the Burghölzli Hospital, he and his colleagues were, of course, familiar with the scientific atmosphere of the time. They were concerned with improving the treatment of their patients, but were far from accepting the traditional outlook on custodial care; they wanted to understand the patient as well as the illness. Research was in the foreground, although results were often disappointing. No doubt—as we can see now—the disappointment in research, such as studying *post-mortem* sections of the brain, was brought about by the all-important place given to causation. A cure for mental illness, so it was thought, was dependent upon discovering its cause.

Even today the significance of causation is often overrated in psychiatry as well as in general medicine. When a diagnosis of neurosis seems certain, it is by no means unusual for the doctor, almost as a matter of conscience, to exclude organic disorder, as though nothing else could produce the symptoms. He has been trained to think of an organic cause as the only important factor in illness, and it is remarkable how much significance can be attributed to any physical illness, small or great, past or present. Everyone knows the importance of diagnosing organic trouble, but equal importance should be given to recognizing disturbances within the mind. A patient goes to his doctor and expects him to find and remove the cause of his illness. In many instances—for example, in infectious diseases—the search for a cause may be successful and administration of the correct remedy may be followed by recovery. Nevertheless, fervent searching for so-called causes can be harmful to the patient by suggesting additional symptoms. Every experienced doctor will see, if he is alive to it, that unfortunate effects may follow the symptomatic or the palliative treatment of symptoms. But he might not agree, because he has not thought of it, that prolonged and fruitless investigations can be disastrous. Patients have their attention focused on the past and become convinced that more complete examinations by more distinguished authorities must at long last reveal the cause. A similar line of thought seems to lie behind the deterministic systems of psychological thought, with treatment involving protracted examination of past events. Scrutiny of past experience and the recovery of lost memories do not in themselves act like magic in producing a cure. Yet this approach is pursued zealously, as though it were the only way.

Neurosis may appear at any age, and if it be assumed that its origin lies in the past, the search for the cause may provide an escape from a present-day problem. Life may be compared to a river: in the early stages there are the little tributaries, and as the river flows on the channel deepens and the side-streams disappear. Should the river be blocked the level rises and water flows back into the old channels. But these old channels (like the experiences in childhood) have not caused the river to rise; the problem is the block in the river. When doctor and patient alike are blind to the present problem, there are always the endless things of childhood to talk about; for childhood is a time of phantasies. The so-called scientific procedure based only on causality without taking into account the relevance of the present situation is likely to prove disappointing in discovering a cure for mental illness. But tradition dies hard. Learning is difficult enough, but how hard it is to unlearn!

With growing experience, Jung came to adopt a wider approach than his contemporaries; he came to see that causes in the past, however important, were not the only consideration in illness. There was also response to the present situation and the patient's attitude towards future responsibilities. He felt that the illness was serving some purpose; that there was a goal, even though its nature was unknown. Mental illness, like life itself, had an aim, a meaning. He knew the importance of the personal history, and he would never attempt to treat a patient without finding out the setting, the background, in which illness had developed; but in addition to investigation of the past he took into account the present and the future. Insight into experiences and the recovery of repressed memories are highly important; but this does not mean that specific causes of the illness must be found. Adjustment and cure are in the present, not in the long-past days of childhood. It was relevant also to consider why the person got ill in that particular way and at that time. If the illness resulted only from past events, why had it not come earlier?

The often fruitless, almost microscopic, examination of the past receives a healthy corrective in Jung's emphasis on the present and on the future. This gives prominence also to a feature in the evolutionary outlook which is sometimes overlooked: that evolution is a process, and each phenomenon, in addition to its past and present, should be expressed or considered in terms of its future possibilities if these can be inferred. Important though origins may be, in themselves they can be meaningless when the present situation and the coming days and years must be faced. 'Where do we go from here?' trite as it is, contains a truth.

It comes as a surprise to find support for Jung's ideas from psychiatrists whom one must suppose are not familiar with his work, otherwise they would certainly have referred to it. Dr. Franz Alexander[1] writes as follows: '. . . we lay stress on the value of designing a *plan of treatment*, based on a dynamic-diagnostic appraisal of the patient's personality and the actual problems he has to solve in his given life conditions . . .'. Dr. T. M. French says much the same thing: 'The more we keep our attention focused upon the patient's immediate problem in life, the more clearly do we come to realize that the patient's neurosis is an unsuccessful attempt to solve a problem in the present by means of behaviour patterns that failed to solve it in the past. We are interested in the past as a source of these sterotyped behaviour patterns, but our primary interest is in helping the patient to find a solution for his present problem. . . .'

These are extracts from a book by a group of psychoanalysts who claim that all of their work is a development of Freud's. Many other clinical procedures in Alexander and French's valuable book have been used by Jungian analysts for many years.

'Life', writes Jung, 'is teleology *par excellence*; it is the intrinsic striving towards a goal, and the living organism is a system of directed aims which seek to fulfil themselves. The end of every process is its goal. Youthful longing for the world and for life, for the attainment of high hopes and distant goals, is life's obvious teleological urge which at once changes into fear of life, neurotic resistances, depression, and phobias if at some point it remains caught in the past, or shrinks from risks without which the unseen goal cannot be attained.'[2]

Another principle of explanation, of understanding, in addition to the importance of the current situation and the goal-seeking char-

1. Alexander, F., and French, T. M., *Psychoanalytic Therapy*, Ronald Press (1946), pp. 5, 95.
2. *The Structure and Dynamics of the Psyche* (1960), C. W., Vol. 8, p. 406.

acteristics of life, arises from the observation that an event may occur in what is to us a meaningful association with another event of a like kind. We have been accustomed to describe as coincidence events existing or happening at the same time, indicating only that causality linking these events has not been observed. Every doctor has had experience of diagnosing an unusual type of illness, one he may not have seen for years; yet on the same day he comes across one or two other patients with the identical complaint. We describe such events as odd, curious, remarking inconclusively (and inaccurately), 'It never rains but it pours.'

Jung employs the term 'synchronicity' of ' "coincidences" connected so meaningfully that their "chance" concurrence would represent a degree of improbability that would have to be expressed by an astronomical figure.'[3]

Teilhard de Chardin, writing from a very different angle, using other concepts, expressed ideas which seem to converge towards Jung's: '. . . the unknown . . . disguised its presence in the innumerable strands which form the web of chance, the very stuff of which the universe and my own small individuality are woven. . . . Our mind is disturbed when we try to plumb the depth of the world beneath us. But it reels still more when we try to number the favourable chances which must coincide at every moment if the least of living things is to survive and to succeed in its enterprises. After the consciousness of being something other and something greater than myself—a second thing made me dizzy: namely, the supreme improbability, the tremendous unlikelihood of finding myself existing in the heart of a world that has survived and succeeded in being a world.'[4]

Dissatisfaction with the causal principle was plainly stated by Jung in the Preface to a volume first published in 1917: 'But causality is only one principle, and psychology cannot be exhausted by causal methods only, because the mind lives by aims as well. . . .

'To interpret Faust objectively, i.e. from the causal standpoint,

3. *Ibid.*, p. 437.
4. Teilhard de Chardin, Pierre, *Le Milieu Divin*, Collins (1960), p. 56.

is as though a man were to consider a sculpture from the historical, technical and—last but not least—from the mineralogical standpoint. But where lurks the *real meaning* of the wondrous work?'[5]

We note, then, that Jung's 'heresy respecting causality', as it was called, was a step in his search for an explanatory principle, for he was really dissatisfied with the exclusiveness of the statistical method. Next came the notion of directed aims—'the aim of every process is its goal'—and in addition to these is 'the problem of synchronicity' with which Jung was concerned for many years; but the difficulties of the problem and its presentation deterred him until 1952 when he published a consistent account of everything he had to say on the subject. With some revisions, this work has now been re-published.[6]

As we might expect after so many years of thought, Jung's observations on 'Synchronicity: An Acausal Connecting Principle' are presented with due circumspection: 'Although meaningful coincidences are infinitely varied in their phenomenology, as acausal events they nevertheless form an element that is part of the scientific picture of the world. Causality is the way we explain the link between two successive events. Synchronicity designates the parallelism of time and meaning between psychic and psychophysical events, which scientific knowledge so far has been unable to reduce to a common principle.'[7] There are exceptions to the general concept in physics or space, time and causality, and it is here that synchronicity acquires a meaning.

Jung's interest in the meaning and explanatory possibilities of the synchronicity concept long ago led him to investigate for himself aspects of Chinese thought contained in *The I Ching or Book of Changes*.[8] For thousands of years, he tells us,[9] the best minds of

5. Jung, C. G., *Collected Papers on Analytical Psychology*, Baillière, Tindall, and Cox (1920), pp. xv, 340.
6. *The Structure and Dynamics of the Psyche* (1960), C. W., Vol. 8, p. 419.
7. *Ibid.*, pp. 530, 531.
8. *The I Ching or Book of Changes*, translated by Richard Wilhelm, rendered into English by Cary F. Baynes, Foreword by C. G. Jung, two volumes, Routledge and Kegan Paul (1951).
9. *The Secret of the Golden Flower*, translated and explained by Richard Wilhelm, with a European Commentary by C. G. Jung. Kegan Paul, Trench, Trübner (1931), pp. 141, 142.

China have contributed to this remarkable book; yet despite its fabulous age, it has never grown old, but lives and operates still, at least for those who understand its meaning. 'The science of the *I Ching* is not based on the causality principle, but on a principle (hitherto unnamed because not met with among us) which I have tentatively called the *synchronistic* principle.' It was in his memorial address for Richard Wilhelm that Jung first used the term 'synchronicity'.[10]

This famous book, *I Ching*, is sometimes disposed of as a collection of Chinese magic spells, but only by those who have never turned its pages or investigated its possibilities. Richard Wilhelm, the sinologue, describes it as one of the most important books in the world's history. In his Foreword[11] to Wilhelm's translation, Jung writes: 'This odd fact that a reaction that makes sense arises out of a technique seemingly excluding all sense from the outset, is the great achievement of the *I Ching*.' Although we may not, as yet, be able to prove certain items of knowledge reached by an unfamiliar method, such as the wisdom of the *I Ching*, as Jung has said, this, in itself, should not lead us to conclude that it is all nonsense; there may be truth of an unknown kind, and it may be true on a basis unknown to us. As reasonable people we must admit that its rationale is mysterious for we do not know how it works, but we observe that it does so, and often it can give an amazing insight into character. This is the important thing: certainly not whether the *I Ching* is true or false by our particular code of reasoning. Such a standpoint may baffle the intellectualist demanding proof of every proposition before accepting it. Yet who would try to prove the truth or falsity of mythology? Surely only he who is thinking of proof as it is used in a court of law or in circles where the scientific method is inviolable. Jung would think it a waste of time to discuss whether or not a myth was true; for him a main feature in mythology is that myths are repeated; that this is so will not be disputed.

10. *The Structure and Dynamics of the Psyche* (1960), C. W., Vol. 8, p. 452.
11. *The I Ching or Book of Changes*, translated by Richard Wilhelm, rendered into English by Cary F. Baynes, Foreword by C. G. Jung (1951), Vol. I, p. ix.

Likewise with astrology. Again and again I have been asked if Jung 'really believes in astrology'. This is an understandable question, for Jung has written much about the subject, and everyone knows the status of astrology in the minds of thoughtful people. But how many have read what he has written? Strangers sometimes write to Jung arguing to show that astrology is nonsense and supplying information about changes in the calendar and so forth. 'Bringing owls to Athens'—the ancient form of 'bringing coals to Newcastle'—was his comment on these well-meaning correspondents. He told me in so many words that he did not concern himself with the truth or falsity of astrology. By 'truth' is here meant a conclusion derived in a logical manner from the axioms—that is, the simple propositions on which it rests. Thus the axioms of Euclid's geometry, if accepted, would provide a criterion of truth. Whether or not astrology is true is of no interest to Jung. He has no illusions about the imperfections of astrology and no doubt that it would cut a poor figure under scientific inspection. He knows that the claims of astrology cannot be 'proved'; but of more significance would be an explanation of how it ever works, how it could ever give a hint. That it does so cannot be disputed. Jung at one time thought the results of astrological observation might be regarded as synchronistic phenomena; but it is conceivable that there may be a causal basis for astrology, and if this is even 'remotely thinkable, synchronicity becomes an exceedingly doubtful proposition'.[12]

When Jung began his career as a psychiatrist he set no bounds to his work. Preconceived ideas were left behind; his mind was never 'clogged with prudence'—to quote R. L. S.—and his outlook was constantly expanding.

Perplexity concerning the symbolism of dreams and other unconscious occurrences led Jung to embark on the study of alchemy. This proved highly fruitful. Somewhat to his surprise, he discovered that the alchemists were concerned with psychological and religious problems not very different from those of his patients.

12. *The Structure and Dynamics of the Psyche* (1960), C. W., Vol. 8, pp. 460, 461.

Moreover, their understanding of these problems was often profound. Alchemy flourished for many centuries in the East and in the West, so, naturally, not every alchemist was a paragon. Jung has built up what is probably the finest library of alchemical texts in Switzerland and he has read every one of them. Consequently, his remarks on this obscure subject are soundly based. It is unnecessary for our present purpose to do more than refer the reader to Jung's writings in *Psychology and Alchemy*[13] and in the two volumes, *Mysterium Coniunctionis*.[14] Of special importance is the Introduction to the former book *Introduction to the Religious and Psychological Problems of Alchemy*.[15] One extract from the book may be given: 'The central ideas of Christianity are rooted in gnostic philosophy, which, in accordance with psychological laws, simply *had* to grow up at a time when the classical religions had become obsolete. It was founded on the perception of the symbols thrown up by the process of individuation which always sets in when the collective dominants of human life fall into decay. At such a time there is bound to be a considerable number of individuals who are possessed by archetypes of a numinous nature that force their way up to the surface in order to form new dominants.'[16]

Jung's researches in the obscure hinterland of the human mind were possible because he was unhampered by the bonds of a purely personalistic psychology. It was the striking applicability of the hypothesis of the collective unconscious that opened up so many unexpected possibilities, and the great help alchemical symbolism gives to the understanding and interpretation of dreams as well as of the peripatetic qualities of the individuation process.

13. *Psychology and Alchemy* (1953), C. W., Vol. 12.
14. *Mysterium Coniunctionis* (1963), C. W., Vol. 14.
15. *Psychology and Alchemy*, *op. cit.*, p. 3.
16. *Ibid.*, p. 35.

CHAPTER EIGHT

Aion: The Mind in Time

WE now turn to a remarkable book which Jung published in 1950.[1] In it familiar psychological concepts find little place; but this does not mean that they have lost their importance. The therapeutic situation is what it is and nothing in Jung's later work displaces his earlier teaching on psychology and psychopathology. He is now, as he has always been, emphatic that psychiatrists, particularly those engaged in analytical work, should have a wide experience in general medicine as well as in psychiatry. Life opens out before Jung in all sorts of unexpected ways, and in his later books he assumes that his readers are not beginners. *Aion* is a profound book; no one could say it was a book to be read at a sitting.

Not all of Jung's books have been translated into English, and it has not been expedient to do more than mention briefly the individuation process on which he lays particular emphasis. But those who read *Aion* carefully should note that Jung sees it as representing the collective aspect of the individuation process.

To give the reader an impression of the scope of this volume, and through it a glimpse of Jung's more recent work, a critical notice—that is, a review—of the book from *the Journal of Analytical Psychology*[2] follows.

1. *Aion: Researches into the Phenomenology of the Self* (1959), C. W., Vol. 9, Part II.
2. Bennet, E. A., 'Jung's Concept of the Time Stream', *Journal of Analytical Psychology* (1960), Vol., 5, p. 159.

I

Aion, that is, an era, a segment of historical time, bears the mark of Jung's fully mature mind. His early books and those of middle life were written with precision. Often the substance was complex—nature usually is!—but the exposition, for instance of dreams, was easily assimilated. Few will find this book easy to read and some may lay it aside. That is understandable; but the hesitant may start again if they reflect that Jung, now in his later years, feels it a duty, an obligation, to record his reflections and observations upon unusual and generally unnoticed psychological phenomena. He has gone to immense trouble, by detailed documentation and collation, to support his theme, and as always, he has been careful to avoid unjustifiable assumptions—let alone draw conclusions—which might imply a claim to absolute truth. Those who are interested to know what he has to say in this profound book must be prepared to read, to re-read and to ponder.

Some readers will be mystified by the frontispiece, depicting the Mithraic god Aion, and possibly this has already puzzled some reviewers; at all events it has come in for little comment. No explanation is given for the choice of this plate; yet understanding the import of this god gives a hint about the intention of the book as well as its title. Many Mithraic statues of Aion have survived, and the illustration used here is of one in the Vatican Library collection. The god is seen in the likeness of a human monster with the head of a lion—this probably relates to the summer season—and the body enveloped by a serpent. According to Cumont,[3] the statues of Aion are decorated with numerous symbols in keeping with the kaleidoscopic nature of his character. Objects carried in the hands vary: some show the sceptre and the bolts of divine sovereignty or in each hand a key, as proper for the monarch of the heavens whose portals he opens. The wings are symbolic of the rapidity of his flight, and also suggest the air. He stands on a globe representing the earth, encircled by the folds of a snake typifying the tortuous course of the

3. Cumont, Franz, *The Mysteries of Mithra*, Dover Publications (1956), pp. 107 *et seq.*

sun on the ecliptic. Celestial and terrestrial phenomena signalizing the eternal flight of the years are brought to mind by the signs of the zodiac engraved on his body and the emblems of the seasons that accompany them. Sometimes a serpent is around each of his wings. Aion creates and destroys all things; he is the lord and master of the four elements that compose the universe, and he may be identified with Destiny.

Aion has had many names, acquired fortuitously or established by convention: thus he is synonymous with the Mithraic god Kronos (the Greek name for Saturn), sometimes referred to as *saeculum* (the spirit of the age, the times) or more expressively, boundless, infinite time.

Dozens of meanings have been given to the word 'time': it may refer to duration set out by measure; to a space of time apart from divisions into hours or years; to a subjective form of perceiving phenomena; to the length of a term of imprisonment; and so on. Jung's concern is to see time in its historical setting, that is, the emphasis is upon prevailing conditions of mind at stages within the period, the era, about which he is writing. People change as the time(s) changes; the one varies with the other for they are inseparable, and each in its way expresses an underlying entity. Hence Jung's choice of the frontispiece, for Aion is the symbol of the creative qualitative principle of time.

Dr. Marie-Louise von Franz's *Analysis of the Passion of St. Perpetua*[4] *(Die Passion S. Perpetuae)* appears in the German edition, and in some ways this is an integral part of *Aion*, for it describes the psychological phenomena which accompanied the transformation of the old Pagan world into the early Christian mentality. Christianity at that time came out of the collective unconscious by way of dreams and visions; it did not fall from heaven by direct revelation. Consequently, to obey one's unconscious meant to become a Christian. St. Perpetua's dreams show the transformation of unconscious collective representations from paganism to Christianity. It should not be thought that the dreams of today—that is, 2,000 years later—would show a similar ten-

4. St. Perpetua; A.D. 181–206.

dency. Dr. von Franz also cited evidence indicating that Christ at that time was an *inner* figure appearing in dreams. Jung's claim that Christ was a projection of the self is thus confirmed. Aion deals with the beginning of this transformation of Christian ideas, and this is followed by the succession of events from the early days and through the Middle Ages to modern times. Psychological changes in individuals (and so in groups), characteristic of the transition from one era or period of time to another, provide the leitmotiv. If this is kept in mind, some difficult passages will be made clear.

To outline on a conscious level the changes in the time stream over the centuries would have its value. But Jung has chosen another approach, and that is to consider the historical transformations by means of a critical investigation of distinctive phenomena due to unconscious processes. These, he points out, always accompany the fluctuations of consciousness. No one living in the West can escape the historical Christian background or avoid being influenced by the secular changes in Christian principles. In a striking passage we get a picture of how Christianity has altered, and Jung reaches the conclusion that statements of Christian principles, such as those by Paul in the market place at Athens, which had a remarkable effect when first made, have little meaning for people today. He writes:

'If Paul were alive today, and should undertake to reach the ear of intelligent Londoners in Hyde Park, he could no longer content himself with quotations from Greek literature and a smattering of Jewish history, but would have to accommodate his language to the intellectual faculties of the modern English public. If he failed to do this he would have announced his message badly, for no one, except perhaps a classical philologist, wound understand half of what he was saying. That, however, is the situation in which Christian kerygmatics (preaching or declaration of religious truth) finds itself today. Not that it uses a dead foreign language in the literal sense, but it speaks in images that on the one hand are hoary with age and look deceptively familiar, while on the other hand they are miles away from a modern man's conscious understanding, addressing themselves, at most to his unconscious, and then only if the speaker's whole soul is in the work' (pp. 177–78).

Some will accept, others dispute this comment. But that there is truth in it could hardly be denied.

II

Developments that have taken place over the years are only possible when the individual—that is, many individuals—are transforming themselves in their personal psychological life, and the phenomenology may be individual or it may be collective. Thus knowledge concerning the manifestation of symbols may be of a single symbol or of symbols expressing a general disposition, as in myths. The latter disposition is the collective unconscious, 'the existence of which can be inferred only from individual phenomenology. In both cases (that is, the individual and the collective) the investigator comes back to the individual, for what he is all the time concerned with are certain complex thought-forms, the archetypes, and they must be conjectured as the unconscious organisers of our ideas. The motive force that produces these configurations cannot be distinguished from the trans-conscious factor known as instinct. There is, therefore, no justification for visualising the archetype as anything other than the image of the instinct' (p. 179). It should be remembered that 'the word "image" expresses the contents of the unconscious momentarily constellated. . . . The interpretation of its meaning, therefore, can proceed exclusively neither from the unconscious nor from the conscious, but only from their reciprocal relation.'[5]

Aion opens with what seems at first glance to be an admirable and simple exposition of the ego, the shadow, the syzygy (the paired opposites anima and animus), and the self. But with closer reading it will be noted that these terms are being discussed from the point of view of feeling, and feeling is evidently more in place than thinking: '. . . the intellectual "grasp" of a psychological fact produces no more than a name. . . . It would seem that one can pursue any science with the intellect alone except psychology whose subject—the

5. *Psychological Types*, Kegan Paul, Trench, Trübner (1933), p. 555.

psyche—has more than the two aspects mediated by sense-perception and thinking. The function of value—feeling—is an integral part of our conscious orientation. . . . It is through the "affect" that the subject becomes involved and comes to feel the whole weight of reality. The difference amounts roughly to that between a severe illness which one reads about in a text-book and the real illness which one has' (pp. 32, 33). We also find in these chapters the first steps in Jung's elucidation of the numerous aspects of the archetype of the self. The 'shadow' containing the hidden, repressed and more or less nefarious part of the personality has usually been presented as the shadow cast by the conscious mind—that is, a phenomenon relating primarily to the personal psychology. In this guise it is easily understood. But here it carries this connotation, and also the wider notion of everything that is unconscious. So it 'proves to be a darkness that hides influential and autonomous factors which can be distinguished in their own right—namely, animus and anima' (p. 266). So the shadow contains more than regrettable tendencies: it has good qualities—normal instincts, creative impulses, and so on—and evil is seen as a misapplication of facts in themselves natural. These personifications now appear as anima and animus, and these are the real authors of evil. In fact all the archetypes develop favourable and unfavourable effects. And because there can be no reality without polarity, the self is seen as a *complexio oppositorum* (pp. 266, 267).

Jung's emphasis on feeling is another way of saying that certain psychological formulations can only be substantiated in the mind of the individual by means of his own experience of them; unless we have a personal experience of so-called realities they mean nothing to us. Those who have travelled by air know something which is unknown to those who have never been in an aeroplane; the personal experience can be described, but it cannot be felt by another unless he makes a journey by air. Jung's emphasis upon feeling may arouse criticism; yet without feeling comprehension is incomplete, and comprehension for most people follows training. Trite though this may sound, it offends some who consider that training in Analytical Psychology (or in psychoanalysis for that matter) automatically produces conditioned devotees incapable of judgment. Such shallow reasoning would not be levelled at consulting engineers or even at physicians. But then criticism of these callings does not involve the emotion of the critic. Again and again Jung has explained the nature of his experiences and the method of obtaining them. Those who have used his methods have confirmed the facts he has described. 'One could see the moons of Jupiter even in Galileo's day if one took the trouble to use his telescope' (pp. 33–34). Outside the field of psychology there is no difficulty in understanding such concepts as the shadow or the anima or the self. Thus the anima/animus combination has been described in literature before Jung's day, as anyone can confirm by reading, for example, Hardy's *Well-Beloved*, published when Jung was a schoolboy. As already mentioned, Jung was interested in alchemy because he found in it experiences parallel to those he came across in the treatment of patients. Likewise, 'the self, on account of its empirical peculiarities, proves to be the *eidos* behind the supreme ideas of unity and totality that are inherent in all monotheistic and monistic systems' (p. 34).

III

In the Prefatory Note to *Answer to Job*[6] Jung writes: 'The most immediate cause of my writing this book is perhaps to be found in certain problems discussed in my book, *Aion*, especially the problem of Christ as a symbolic figure and of the antagonism Christ-Antichrist, represented in the traditional zodiacal symbolism of the two fishes.' Linked with this statement is Jung's theory that the symbol of the self undergoes a transformation over the centuries, so that in every astrological or platonic year (2,150 years) another form appears. As signs of the zodiac are enumerated anti-clockwise, the bull would (roughly) cover the era 4000 to 2000 B.C. and likewise the ram 2000 to 0 B.C., and next comes the aeon of Pisces, A.D. 0 to 2000. Of this period the first 1,000 years (A.D. 0 to 1000) is held to represent the first fish of Pisces, i.e. Christ, and the second 1,000

6. *Psychology and Religion: West and East* (1958), C. W., Vol. II, p. 357.

years (A.D. 1000 to 2000) the second fish, that is, Antichrist. An enormous number of synchronistic events throughout history reflect this strange sequence of constellations. Ignorance is often coupled with distrust and scorn of astrological concepts. But sensible people—by their standards—paid a lot of attention to the stars in their courses at the beginning of the Christian era and for thousands of years before it. Such material about astrology will not come up to the standards of the scientist (including the psychologist) whose methodology is irrevocably imbued with the notion of causality. All such should know that Jung is not writing in support of astrology. His concern is with the mental outlook of thoughtful people who lived nearly 2,000 years ago. The ways of the mind in the early days of Christianity were not static; we see movement and alteration in the human psyche and this movement in the 'stream of the centuries' (p. 173) is active in our own day and generation. About these concepts and events Jung is not dogmatic. True to his rôle of empirical psychologist, he correlates the facts and produces a hypothesis which seems to offer an explanation. 'Inevitably, we move here on uncertain ground and must now and then have recourse to a speculative hypothesis or tentatively reconstruct the context' (p. 269).

That Jung is not writing for the novice—psychological or theological—is evident when we consider his commentary on Christ as a symbol of the self: 'The images of God and Christ which man's religious fantasy projects cannot avoid being anthropomorphic and are admitted to be so; hence they are capable of psychological elucidation like any other symbols' (p. 67). In this non-theological setting Christ as the true image of God exemplifies the archetype of the self (p. 37), and as such is a proper subject for psychological reflection. A statement such as that of St. Augustine: 'Therefore our end must be our perfection, but our perfection is Christ', would find its psychological equivalent in the integration of the collective unconscious which forms an essential part of the individuation process. Clearly Jung is not discussing in this context the relative simplicities of personal psychology, but is touching on the fundamental entities behind the individual. The image of the Antichrist—that is, 'the Luciferian development of science and technology and the frightful material and moral destruction left behind by the Second World War' (p. 36)—appears as the dark aspect of the self. Here are the irreconcilable opposites, the insoluble conflicts of duty (pp. 44–5) already mentioned (p. 25) or more simply that 'good and evil represent equivalent halves of an opposition' (p. 45). Individuation becomes the prominent task, and not at all as a circumvention of the Christian mystery (p. 70). There is here no theological discussion; Jung disclaims any missionary intentions (p. 68), but is concerned to express the fact that as Christ is taken as a symbol of the self it does not follow that perfection and completeness are identical. So too the individual striving after perfection will experience the opposite of his conscious intentions, and this in its turn is just how life (rather than stagnation and death) appears; conflict can never be far away.

In Chapter VI, 'The Sign of the Fishes', and in the following chapters the argument or exposition of this theme continues.

Jung in dealing with the phenomenology of the self notes the facts as he sees them. He did not invent the ideas and the turn of expression found in astrology about the Fishes. There they are, plain for everyone to see. Some brush them aside; Jung takes them seriously as facts to be observed in his efforts to elucidate what has happened, and what is happening today, in the development of self—that is, the hypostasized entity behind the innumerable manifestations and projections of those far-off years up to our own time. To Jung the unfolding of history has a meaning; to others it may be merely boring, stupid or fancy running free. Further, he thinks the meaning is important, otherwise he would not have attempted the almost superhuman task of elucidating it. Nor is he the first to do so: 'What I have described as a gradual process of development has already been anticipated, and more or less prefigured at the beginning of our era' (p. 184). Here the reference is to the images and ideas in Gnosticism, to which Chapter XIII is devoted. Modern psychology is not responsible for the notion of the unconscious: the Gnostics had the idea of an unconscious and in particular the initial unconsciousness of man (pp. 190–1). Further, Jung considers that the same concept was found in St. Paul's teaching where the transformation from unconsciousness took on a moral tone: to sin, to repent, alludes to 'the times of ignorance', that is, unconsciousness. Much of the work of the Gnostics has a modern flavour and symbols of the self are numerous. Jung's account of Gnostic symbolic thinking is more easily grasped than the preceding chapters on the historical, alchemical and other aspects of the fish. The purpose is 'to give the reader a picture of the mentality of the first two centuries of our era'. The partly pagan, partly Christian views of the Gnostics show how closely the religious teaching of that age was connected with psychic facts (p. 215).

Chapter XIV, 'The Structure and Dynamics of the Self', gives a summary of the progressive assimilation and amplification of the archetype that underlies ego-consciousness. Knowing (or guessing) the pitfalls due to differences in outlook over the centuries, Jung is almost bound 'to venture an occasional hypothesis even at the risk of making a mistake' (p. 269). Surely a modestly disarming understatement! A highly condensed chapter follows, packed with facts, theories and frank guesses, and this will be hard going for some. But they need not regret the absence of tabulated findings. Jung describes the entire book as 'a mere sketch', and there is some truth in this.

Symbolism has undergone development from one age to another, for, like everything in life, symbols have their day and cease to be. In this transitional setting we are given in outline the facts that led psychologists to conjecture an archetype of wholeness, that is, the self (p. 223). In other words the book is the archetypal history of the mind in the Christian aeon (p. 227). Alchemy succeeded gnostic philosophy and ' "Mater Alchemia" is one of the mothers of modern science with its unparalleled knowledge of the "dark" side of matter . . . and in the twentieth century political and social "realism" has turned the wheel of history back a full two thousand years' (pp. 232–3).

'Man's picture of the world during the second millenium includes the beginning of natural science', and this brings to the fore the principle of correspondence, widely recognized up to the time of Leibniz. Elsewhere Jung has expanded on the need to supplement our time-conditioned thinking 'by the principle of correspondence, or as I have called it, synchronicity' (p. 258).

Nuclear physics and the psychology of the unconscious may

seem to have little in common, but each body of knowledge—one with the concept of the atom, the other with that of the archetype—seem to be moving into transcendental territory, and Jung hints that they may draw closer. At the same time he is fully aware of the extremely hypothetical nature of his reflections. Yet psyche and matter exist in one and the same world and each partakes of the other, otherwise any reciprocal action would be impossible. Speculative ideas, such as his, find a place in all analogy formation and, as Jung has shown elsewhere (*Psychology and Alchemy*), analogy formation can be observed in its countless forms everywhere in history and its importance cannot be questioned.

Jung would not claim that in *Aion* he had done more than give a hint, a foreshadowing of coming events as a new era dawns. His modesty should not be allowed to diminish the importance he assigns to the historical changes which are becoming more and more evident. In fact, he returns to this subject in a later publication.[7] 'What will the future bring? From time immemorial this question has occupied men's minds.' These opening words of the book show that, once more, Jung is concerned with issues that go far beyond the boundaries of psychology and psychiatry. What, he asks,[8] is the significance of that split, symbolized by the 'Iron Curtain', which divides humanity into two halves? He sees scientific education, based in the main on statistical truths and abstract knowledge, and the individual regarded as a merely marginal phenomenon and, ultimately, the State as the principle of political reality.

The prevailing tendency to seek the source of all ills in the outside world leads to the demand for political and social changes which it is supposed would automatically solve the much deeper problem of split personality[9] or 'split consciousness' characteristic of the mental disorder of our day. Jung is here thinking of modern society rather than individuals, for he sees 'society' acting as if it were an individual, as when the individual loses himself, disappears

7. *The Undiscovered Self*, Routledge and Kegan Paul (1958).
8. *Ibid*, pp. 3. 11, 12.
9. *Ibid.*, pp. 74, 80.

in so far as he allows himself to be submerged in the mass. He was intrigued to learn from one of his granddaughters that she and a group of her contemporaries had been discussing the essays in his little book. Their comments were very much to the point. He was particularly interested to observe the acute perception of these schoolgirls; to his mind, the younger generation appeared to have a clearer, more intelligent view of the world situation than their elders, who are limited by the tendency to see the world today as if nothing had changed and as if matters were bound to settle down.

Jung does not share this complacency. Humanity, he considers, is passing through a difficult, dark time, and inevitably there will be psychological accompaniments. Now, in our day we are given 'a golden opportunity to see how a legend is formed' at such a time; how a miraculous tale grows up of an attempted intervention by extra-terrestrial 'heavenly bodies'. This is the theme of a second small volume on the subject of *Flying Saucers,*[10] first published in 1959. Bertrand Russell expressed a similar idea: 'And a dose of disaster is likely to bring men's hopes back to their older super-terrestrial forms: if life on earth is despaired of, it is only in heaven that peace can be sought.'[11]

UFOs (unidentified flying objects) have been reported from all corners of the earth. Although the UFOs were first publicized only towards the end of the Second World War, the same phenomenon was known earlier.[12] In support of this, illustrations are reproduced of similar objects printed in the *Nuremberg Broadsheet* in 1561 and in the *Basel Broadsheet* in 1566. A 'very frightful spectacle' seen by 'numerous men and women' at sunrise on 14th April, 1561 has much in common with the UFOs of today: 'Globes of a blood-red, bluish or black colour' or 'plates' in large number near the sun. . . . Moreover, there were 'two great tubes'. 'They all began to fight one another. . . .' Underneath the globes a long object was seen, 'shaped

10. *Flying Saucers: A Modern Myth of Things Seen in the Skies*, Routledge and Kegan Paul (1959).
11. Russell, Bertrand, *History of Western Philosophy*, George Allen and Unwin (1946), p. 64.
12. *Flying Saucers*, *op. cit.*, pp. 128 *et seq.*

like a great white spear'. Naturally, this spectacle was interpreted as a divine warning.

Jung is not concerned with investigating the reliability[13] of the numerous reports on the UFO phenomena, for his essay is a study of UFOs as a psychological phenomenon. It is quite right that the rumours should meet with criticism, scepticism, and often rejection. . . . Indeed, since conscious and unconscious fantasy, and even mendacity, obviously play an important rôle in building up the rumour, we could be satisfied with a psychological explanation and let it rest at that. Unfortunately, adds Jung, there are good reasons why the UFOs cannot be disposed of in this simple manner, for they have not only been seen, but have also been picked up on the radar screen and have left traces on the photographic plate. . . . No satisfying scientific explanation of even one authentic UFO report has yet been given despite many efforts. . . . 'It boils down to nothing less than this: that either psychic projections throw back a radar echo, or else the appearance of real objects affords an opportunity for mythological projections.' The conclusion is: *something is seen but one doesn't know what.* It is difficult, if not impossible, to form any correct idea of these objects, because they behave not like bodies but like weightless thoughts.[14]

Of particular interest is the fact that not only have UFOs been seen, but, as might be expected, they have also been dreamt about. Jung has devoted a chapter to UFOs in dreams,[15] for only with the unconscious associative context is it possible to make a judgment on the psychic situation constellated by the object.

Bearing in mind the psychological ideas engendered by causation, synchronicity, astrology, alchemy, and last, 'the modern myth of things seen in the Skies', it is not difficult to appreciate the widened outlook which followed Jung's valuation of the psyche, conscious and unconscious.

13. *Ibid.*, pp. 146 *et seq.*
14. *Ibid.*, p. xiii, xiv.
15. *Ibid.*, p. 25.

CHAPTER NINE

I. Dreams
II. The Interplay of Opposites: Individuation

I. DREAMS

UNLIKE many people who say they never dream, Jung has been a 'good' dreamer from infancy, and his subsequent attitude towards dreams was influenced by the impression made upon him at the time by early dreams. No question of interpretation arose in those days, for the dream was accepted simply as a personal experience. A few of these dreams were discussed earlier;[1] they were arresting then, and when he recalled them, as he often did, their significance had not diminished. Mature reflections and critical scrutiny never upset the belief, derived from his own experience, that dreams had some meaning. This is typical of the introverted thinker for whom the inner world is sharp and clear, as is the outer to the extraverted thinker.

At first glance, the dream is not a promising subject and patients are usually surprised when asked about their dreams. Many say they never dream or that their dreams are ridiculous, meaningless. Dreams have every appearance of being nonsense and the common attitude towards them is understandable. Dean Inge, a highly intelligent person, in writing about a psychological subject, gave an opinion of dream psychology: '. . . studying the *dreams* of patients? From my experience I should say that is

1. p. 10 *et seq.*
2. Personal letter.

bosh.'[2] What must the outlook have been in 1900, when Freud's *Interpretation of Dreams* appeared! Jung read this book appreciatively long before he met Freud, and although at the time, and later, he was unable to accept Freud's dicta on dreams, he always acknowledged that it was his 'great achievement to have put dream-interpretation on the right track'.[3] Before Freud's time, as Jung knew, the deciphering of dreams had fallen into disrepute and was classed with fortune-telling and reading tea cups. Yet in the past dreams were treated with respect, as we can see from the records of dreams in the Bible and the importance accorded to them by physicians for many centuries.

Jung was more reserved than Freud in his statements about dreams. He has no fixed formula, and consequently tries to understand each dream *de novo,* with the co-operation of the dreamer; without this, although he might have an impression about the meaning of a dream, he would feel uncertain whether he was correct.

Freud was more downright. Indeed, his rediscovery of the dream came from his thoroughgoing deterministic approach; he examined dreams as a nineteenth-century scientist would investigate any obscure phenomenon: it was a challenge, a mystery to be unravelled, and, if possible, an explanation should be found. Freud gave a biological explanation of the dream: its purpose was to preserve sleep. Sleep may be interrupted by external disturbances, such as noise, or by expressed thoughts evading the censorship—which he postulated—for if the dreamer became aware of these his sleep would be at an end. But he remains asleep because the latent content of the dream is transformed by specific mechanisms into the innocuous form which appears to him. When the dream was analysed it was always possible to see that it expressed a repressed wish. Freud's confidence in this theory was such that he considered the meaning of many dreams obvious, and, without reference to his patient, he felt he knew what the dream meant: 'Symbols make it possible for us in certain circum-

3. *Structure and Dynamics of the Psyche* (1958), C. W., Vol. 8, p. 284.

stances to interpret a dream without questioning the dreamer . . . we are often in a position to interpret it straight away; to translate it at sight, as it were.'[4] He did not advocate this procedure, preferring to follow his method of 'free association'. Nevertheless, the direct method of understanding a dream without analysis by free association would seem to follow from Freud's further statement that the relation between the symbol and the thing symbolized is an invariable one.[5]

It seemed to Jung improbable that dreams could always be interpreted in a particular way and from only one point of view such as Freud's wish-fulfilment theory, however broad the meaning of this term. What evidence was there that dreams should always have the same significance? Consciousness was quite intricate, as everyone would agree, and Jung thought it likely that the unconscious was equally if not more complicated. Hence he could not accept the theory that the dream must always be understood as expressing a repressed wish; in other words, that the unconscious is limited in its mode of functioning.

Jung's exposition of dreams has remained consistent all along. He has produced no dogma of their interpretation, nor does he claim that he can find the meaning of every dream on the spot, for dreaming is an involuntary process over which the conscious attitude can have no control. That is why Jung has put dreams—a psychological fact—on a plane with physiological fact.[6] For him the dream is a natural event: he assumes that the dream is what it is and not something else. So he takes the dream exactly as he finds it and tries to understand it and to avoid presuppositions: '. . . we must give up all preconceived opinions when it comes to the analysis and interpretation of the objective psyche, or in other words, the "unconscious". We do not yet possess a general theory of dreams that would enable us to use a deductive method with impunity, any more than we possess a general theory of consciousness from which

4. Freud, S., *Introductory Lectures on Psycho-Analysis*, George Allen and Unwin (1923), p. 127.
5. *Ibid.*, p. 126.
6. *The Practice of Psychotherapy* (1954), C. W., Vol. 16, p. 142.

we can draw inferences. . . . It should therefore be an absolute rule to assume that every dream and every part of a dream is unknown at the onset, and to attempt an interpretation only after carefully taking up the context.'[7] Such an attitude leaves the field of exploration open, whereas the statement of settled principles can be restricting, and implies that we know a great deal about the unconscious and how it is bound to act.

In psychological matters, the question 'Why does it happen?' is not necessarily more productive of results than the other question, 'To what purpose does it happen?' In a paper[8] on the 'Nature of Dreams', Jung put the matter in this form, and at the same time placed the dream 'among the puzzles of medical psychology'. His answer to the second question gives a very general idea of the function of dreams, and that is the formula of 'compensation', which provides a momentary adjustment of one-sidedness, an equalization of disturbed balance. Compensation should be thought of as a process, observable sometimes in a single dream, but clearer in a long series, when the separate acts of compensation arrange themselves into a kind of plan subordinated to a common goal. Jung makes no claim that the notion of the compensatory function of the unconscious is and always will be valid. He puts the idea forward as his subjective point of view, not as a dogma, and gives his reason for considering the psyche as a self-regulating system comparable to the well-known homeostatic mechanisms in the body.

In analysing the dream, the co-operation of the patient is essential; so from the onset the patient is involved in the treatment, and so is the analyst. The joint endeavour of patient and analyst in the investigation of dreams, and in other ways, entails more than the conscious attitude of each: there is also the inevitable participation of the unconscious. Freud was the first to recognize that the relation bore close resemblances to the child-parent situation; he observed that the patient came to look on the

7. *Psychology and Alchemy* (1913), C. W., Vol. 12, pp. 43, 44.
8. *The Structure and Dynamics of the Psyche* (1960), Vol. 8, pp. 281, 287, 289, 290.

analyst as a parent-figure. The direction of feelings and desires towards a new object (the analyst) were described by Freud as 'transference'—that is, a carrying over from one place, or metaphorically from one form, into another. This is an example of projection, an unconscious process whereby we attribute to other people (or even to inanimate objects) subjective contents of any kind, such as hidden motives. This is never an intentional act and the projection disappears when it is discovered that the seemingly objective situation is really subjective.

Volumes have been written about transference; opinions have varied considerably between Freudians and Jungians, and, strangely enough, between Jungians and Jungians. This is not so serious as it might appear, for transference is by no means a simple matter. Nor are its manifestations confined to doctors and patients. Transference situations may appear between those involved in confidential matters—for instance, lawyers and their clients, parsons and parishioners, teachers and pupils.

Further, the transference situation can, so to speak, work both ways: the analyst may also project unrecognized mental contents upon his patients—the so-called counter-transference.

Jung does not consider that transference is always concerned with infantile erotic phantasies, for the patient is now an adult; '. . . understanding of the transference is to be sought not in its historical antecedents but in its purpose'.[9] But its purpose will not be obvious; it must be sought. Transference is spontaneous, unprovoked, and so it cannot be demanded. Neurosis produces a feeling of isolation and a transference may spring up as an attempt to bridge the gap, especially if the patient feels the doctor is remote or lacks understanding.

There has been discussion in psychological circles over the meaning of the terms 'rapport' and 'transference', and it has been argued that the former should be given up as being already contained in transference. On this topic Jung writes: 'By careful examination of his conscious mind you get to know your patient; you establish what the old hypnotists used to call "rapport". This per-

9. *Ibid.*, p. 74.

sonal contact is of prime importance, because it forms the only safe basis from which to tackle the unconscious.'[10]

Transference often shows compulsive qualities which are absent in rapport. Further, the transference may be intense, and this indicates the importance to the patient of the projected material. This is his property, so to speak, and should be returned to him. The projected contents may be personal or impersonal, and it is essential that the therapist should discriminate between these.

Jung in 1946 published a book on the psychology of the transference; this appeared in English in 1954 in a volume, alluded to above, containing essays on kindred subjects.[11] To it the reader is now referred for an authoritative statement upon the important subject of transference.

For Jung the unconscious is always unknown, and, far from being a part of the mind that can be relied upon to behave in a uniform manner, its activity is unpredictable and usually irrational by conscious standards. It is little wonder that the dream is brushed aside. Let us turn, for example, to a type of dream that raises a still unsolved problem—that is, the dream which appears to deal with the future. Such dreams, by no means rare, may possibly complete a pattern when seen in retrospect. But when they occur, they are usually obscure. Jung had a recurrent dream of a large attractive room in his house. In the dream the existence of this room surprised him. It contained a collection of old manuscripts and books. He did not know its meaning at the time, but when he took up the study of alchemy and acquired books similar to those of the dream, the recurrent dream made sense. Dreams of this kind, his own and those of patients, indicated the presence of an anticipatory quality. Jung would not use the word 'prophetic' of such dreams: '. . . they are no more prophetic than a medical diagnosis or a weather forecast. They are merely an anticipatory combination of probabilities which may coincide with the actual behaviour of things but need not necessarily agree in every detail. Only in the latter case can we speak of "prophecy".'[12] Another

10. *The Development of Personality* (1954), C. W., Vol. 17, p. 97.
11. *The Practice of Psychotherapy* (1954), C. W., Vol. 16, p. 164.
12. *The Structure and Dynamics of the Psyche* (1960), C. W., Vol. 8, p. 255.

example of this anticipatory quality occurred in the dream of the medieval house mentioned earlier,[13] and it adumbrated future work on the subject of the collective unconscious.

Dreams of this type are often recorded. That William Temple, formerly Archbishop of Canterbury, had such experiences is evident from a remark in the Preface to his Gifford Lectures: 'All my decisive thinking goes on behind the scenes; I seldom know when it takes place—much of it certainly on walks or during sleep—and I never know the processes which it has followed. Often when teaching I have found myself expressing rooted convictions which until that moment I had no notion that I held. Yet they are genuinely rooted convictions—the response, not of my ratiocinative intellect, but of my whole being, to certain theoretical and practical propositions.'[14]

One of the best-known accounts of anticipatory dreams is that of J. W. Dunne, who held 'That dreams—dreams in general, all dreams, everybody's dreams—were composed of images of past experience and images of future experiences blended together in approximately equal proportions.'[15]

Anticipatory dreams give a hint of the difficulty in formulating a precise theory about dreams. Students are sometimes puzzled that Jung should place dreams centrally in treatment and yet he avoids being dogmatic on the psychology of dreams. It should be remembered that the dream gives only a glimpse of the unconscious, and as the unconscious is by definition the unknown, the dream is not likely to have a meaning which can be read at a glance. Dreams provide one means of coming to terms with the unconscious; and as no two people are identical, the meaning of a dream must be sought in terms of the dreamer.

Knowledge of the dreamer is thus of first importance, for the dream is his product—the dream is the dreamer. However unexpected the dream, it is a subjective experience and points a contrast between the inner world of the mind and the outer world of objects,

13. See p. 88.
14. Matthews, W. R. (and others), *William Temple: An Estimate and an Appreciation*, James Clarke (1946), pp. 10, 11.
15. Dunne, J. W., *An Experiment with Time*. A. & C. Black (1929), p. 54.

animate and inanimate. No question of evidence that the dream was his experience troubles the dreamer. Yet this is important, for unless we know what the dream means for him we can make nothing of it; the significance lies not in the dream *qua* dream, but in who had the dream and in what circumstances. Consequently, the personal history of the patient must be understood, and for this reductive analysis will be necessary. Provided this goes beyond the superficialities of good advice, it is valuable in giving the setting of the individual. But the main value of the treatment is in getting below the surface, in reaching the unconscious, and here dreams will play an important part.

Associations are asked for, so that the context of items in the dream will be understood. However complicated or however simple the dream may appear, it must be approached by way of the dreamer's associations, for these give the pertinent information about the dream. For example, I was told a long dream by a friend—he was not a patient—and in the course of the dream he posted a letter in a pillar-box. He wondered if this had any particular significance, for, although he knew very little about dream interpretation, he had heard that hollow objects into which something can be inserted had a sexual meaning. Before attempting an answer, I inquired about the pillar-box, the letter, and other details. It transpired that the pillar-box in the dream had a special interest for him because it was the oldest pillar-box in the British Isles, and he had written an article about it and other ancient pillar-boxes. On this and other information from his associations, and the general 'atmosphere' of the dream, it was possible to see some purpose in it.

This method of obtaining a description of the separate parts of the dream is named 'amplification'. By studying the component parts—as one would study the composition of any unknown object—and then considering the dream as a whole, we hope to find its meaning, and at the same time an answer to the question: What is the purpose of the dream?

Participation in the analysis of the dream means that the patient is directly involved in the treatment, and that he and his doctor, on equal terms, are trying to solve the enigma of his neurosis. Common sense and good advice, useful though they may be in other circumstances, are disappointing in clearing up the fears and obsessions which can make life a misery. It is a great help to patients with a neurosis when they find they can do something to help themselves. Before an interview with the doctor, they can study their dreams, and often they come to see their significance for themselves. Dreams are not pathological phenomena to be noted only during illness. When the treatment is over and, we hope, the illness cured, patients are encouraged to pay attention to their dreams and their inner life. There is no danger that this will make them introspective. We should avoid thinking of a psychological disability as we think of a physical injury—that is, as something that can be 'cured' and forgotten. Mental life is a process, and the new attitude gained today may grow dim a little later, for the ebb and flow of life means that nothing remains fixed and settled. Consequently, the individual must be prepared to make new adaptations. 'There is no change that is unconditionally valid over a long period of time. Life has always to be tackled anew.'[16]

Co-operation in treatment prepares the way for self-treatment, and this is not merely a preventive measure; it is the adoption of an attitude in which the unconscious as well as the conscious is valid. When this new outlook is achieved life opens up in unexpected ways. This implies an alteration in our customary ideas about the unconscious, and we need a method of reaching the unconscious in addition to dreams. Jung has described such a method—'active imagination'—which means an activation of the imagination. To form images in the mind apart from those derived from external objects is to use our imagination. By spontaneous drawing and painting, modelling, playing a musical instrument, and in other ways, experience shows that the creative activity of the unconscious can be reached. It is a waking method, as dreams are a sleeping method, of getting in touch with the unconscious. That this procedure can be extremely useful has been proved by the results of art therapy, now widely used in psychiatric hospitals.

One danger in using active imagination, as Jung has pointed

16. *The Structure and Dynamics of the Psyche* (1960), C. W., Vol. 8, p. 72.

out, is that '. . . after a certain point of psychic development has been reached, the products of the unconscious are greatly overvalued because they were boundlessly undervalued before'.[17]

Amplification has some similarity to the philological technique of collation, the critical comparison of documents or texts, carried out to establish the meaning of some obscure passage. Supposing we were puzzled by Ophelia's words, 'They say the owl was a baker's daughter', we should employ collation and, as in amplification, we should find out if statements of a like kind appear in legends. Our endeavours, so far as Ophelia's remark goes, would be successful.

Amplification is different from free-association, where conscious control is eliminated as far as possible and the associations are influenced by the unconscious. Eventually these freely associated ideas may lead to the complexes, but this may not give enlightenment about the dream. Reflection on any object or any thought may similarly lead to the complexes and a dream is not required for this purpose. A comparison of the two methods—free-association and amplification—reveals a different valuation of dreams. Jung would contend that the dream has a bearing on the present problem, and this would apply whether or not the dream was clearly linked with the current situation or was of an anticipatory type. In either case the compensatory function of the dream should be discovered.

It is, of course, important to know something of the complexes, but it is more valuable to discover what the unconscious is doing about them—that is, the message of the dream. Because of the central place accorded to dream-interpretation by Jung in analytical treatment, he values amplification as a method.

As a result of work on the Word Association Test, Jung attached considerable importance to the complex as an indicator of unconscious mental activity. Some have found this confusing, and have gone so far as to say that for Jung the complex is more significant than the dream. Thus Dr. Jacobi quotes him as saying that it is not dreams (as Freud believed) but complexes that provide the royal

17. *The Structure and Dynamics of the Psyche* (1960), C. W., Vol. 8, p. 85.

road to the unconscious.[18] These words, Dr. Jacobi writes, indicate the dominant, the central rôle that he (Jung) assigns to the complex in depth psychology.[19]

Dr. Jacobi's quotation suggests that the complex is more important than the dream, and if so, how can we justify the remark just made that the analysis of dreams occupies the central place in Jung's work? To this the answer is clear: The quotation from Jung's book is accurate as far as it goes, but unfortunately some important words are omitted. The full quotation is: 'The *via regia* to the unconscious, however, is not the dream, as he (Freud) thought, but the complex which is the architect of dreams and symptoms.' 'Architect' means the designer of a structure, and so the complex is the architect in the sense that it determines the structure of the dream; it is the hidden emotional content of the dream and so cannot be separated from the dream. In fact, the complexes become personified in the dream and appear as splinter psyches. In another context Jung describes the dream as the emissary of the unconscious.[20] In the 1953 edition of the same work he writes: '. . . the most important method of getting at the pathogenic conflicts is, as Freud was the first to show, through the analysis of dreams.'[21]

Dreams often contain images possessing a symbolic quality. But unfortunately the word 'symbol' has been used in a different sense by Freud and by Jung. It was mentioned in an earlier chapter[22] that Freud considered symbolism as a mode of expression not individually acquired. Nevertheless, for him 'symbol' was synonymous with 'sign' (derived from the Latin *signum*, a sign, token, mark)—that is, an abbreviated expression for something known. Symbolism used in this way implies a conscious choice.

Jung's concept of symbolism is entirely different from this: '. . . the symbol always presupposes that the chosen expression is the best possible description of a relatively unknown fact; a fact, how-

18. *Ibid.*, p. 101.
19. Jacobi, J., *Complex/Archetype/Symbol in the Psychology of C. G. Jung*, Routledge and Kegan Paul (1959), p. 6.
20. *Two Essays on Analytical Psychology* (1953), C. W., Vol. 7, p. 20.
21. *Ibid.*, p. 20.
22. See pp. 93, 95.

ever, which is none the less recognised or postulated as existing'. This is an extract from Jung's definition of 'symbol'.[23] He considers that a symbol is alive only in so far as it is pregnant with meaning. It is therefore quite impossible to make a living symbol, i.e. one that is pregnant with meaning, from known associations. For what is manufactured never contains more than is put into it. . . . Whether a thing is a symbol or not depends chiefly upon the attitude of the consciousness considering it, as for instance, a mind that regards the given fact not merely as such, but also as an expression of the yet unknown. In these circumstances it provokes unconscious participation. It advances and creates life.

From a comparison of the meanings given by Freud and by Jung to the concept 'symbol' the difference between them will be evident. This is more than a confusion in terminology—it indicates diametrically opposed attitudes. It would be true to say that Jung's concept of symbolism, and all that this implied, was an important element in the breakdown of his collaboration with Freud. 'Psychoanalytical symbolism constitutes the exact antithesis of ordinary symbolism . . . whereas the ordinary symbol implies no direct causal relation with what it symbolizes, the Freudian symbol is essentially and by definition an effect of what it symbolizes. Jung is clearly aware of Freud's mistake in applying the term 'symbols' to dreams and to neurotic symptoms.' So writes Dalbiez,[24] who gives the following quotation from Jung:

'Those conscious contents which give us a clue, as it were, to the unconscious backgrounds are by Freud incorrectly termed symbols. These are not true symbols, however, since, according to his teaching, they have merely the rôle of signs or symptoms of the background processes. The true symbol differs essentially from this, and should be understood as the expression of an intuitive perception which can as yet neither be apprehended better not expressed differently.'[25]

23. *Psychological Types*, Kegan Paul, Trench, Trübner (1953), pp. 601 *et seq.*
24. Dalbiez, R., *Psychoanalytical Method and the Doctrine of Freud*, Longmans Green (1941), Vol. II, pp. 102, 103.
25. *Contributions to Analytical Psychology*, Kegan Paul, Trench, Trübner (1928), pp. 231–2.

Dalbiez continues: 'This critique of Jung's reaches the heart of the question. The fact that the psycho-analytical interpretation of dreams has aroused so much opposition is largely due to the confusion created by the use of the word "symbol" in the sense of "index" or "effect-sign".'

Jung's valuation of the symbol is in striking contrast: 'The psychological mechanism that transforms energy is the symbol. . . . So we have every reason to value symbol-formation and to render homage to the symbol as an inestimable means of utilizing the mere instinctual flow of energy for effective work.'[26]

II. THE INTERPLAY OF OPPOSITES: INDIVIDUATION

Jung makes no claim—like the philosophers of old—to have built up a system explaining human thought and human action or that he has gained insight into the meaning of life. His concern is with psychology rather than philosophy, with the mind itself and how it appears to function. Consequently, his aim has been to describe his observations in the hope that the mind in health and 'the intruders of the mind' in sickness may be understood—at least in part.

From time immemorial the interplay of opposites, the reciprocal movement, both of mental and of physical states, has been thought to contain the key to life's enigmas. Polarity, action and reaction, is seen in every part of nature—including the mind. Whether or not the outer universe operates in this fashion may be disputed, but beyond doubt the interplay of opposites occurs within the mind. Ralph Waldo Emerson's essay on 'Compensation' gives a graphic picture of the dualism that underlies nature, including that part of nature we call mind: 'Life invests itself with inevitable conditions which the unwise seek to dodge. The ancient doctrine of Nemesis, as well as the proverbs of all nations, give point to the same theme. All things are double, one against the other; dualism bisects nature so that each thing is a half, and suggests another to make it whole.'

26. *The Structure and Dynamics of the Psyche* (1960), C. W., Vol. 8, pp. 45, 47.

As belief in the principle of opposites has been widespread for centuries, Jung had good reason to conclude that this is one of the main ways in which psychic energy manifests itself. He often mentions Heraclitus, who attached special importance to the mingling of opposites, the perpetual flux, the incessant movement, of which fire is the symbol. Life for Heraclitus was movement, becoming, a ceaseless struggle between contrary forces. Plato and others hotly disputed his philosophic pretensions, but psychology has much to learn from him.

Energy, in Jung's teaching, accompanies or results from this movement of opposites, and this is shown in the self-regulating tendency mentioned in relation to the compensatory function in dreams.[27] In the tension of opposites we build a wider and higher consciousness. 'The meaning and purpose of a problem seems to be not in its solution, but in our working at it incessantly. This alone preserves us from stultification and petrifaction.'[28] We observe, too, the progression and regression of libido in the opening out of life in childhood and youth and its opposite in old age. Similarly, the energy can be thought of as a to-and-fro movement between the levels of consciousness and the personal or the collective unconscious. Likewise, the contrast between conscious and unconscious attitudes can be seen in the dissimilar picture given by the aspect of our personality we present to the world and its counterpart in the unconscious. Jung coined the term 'persona' (literally a mask) for the adopted attitude through which connection is maintained with the outer world, and this may be very different from the 'shadow' side, a term applied to personal and also to collective elements in the unconscious.

Dreams give an indication of the opposites, and the union of the opposites is an important consideration in the treatment of neurosis. Within each of us this other part, the shadow, may be personified in dreams as a stranger; then—if we have eyes to see it—we get a glimpse from the unconscious of what we are pleased to call 'our-

27. See p. 134.
28. *The Structure and Dynamics of the Psyche* (1960), C. W., Vol. 8, p. 394.

selves'. Projection of the shadow occurs almost as a routine and regrettable qualities in ourselves are criticized in others.

Jung's teaching on the psychology of men and of women gives a further contrast: 'They (the sexes) represent a supreme pair of opposites, not hopelessly divided by logical contradiction, but, because of the mutual attraction between them, giving promise of union and actually making it possible.'[29]

The inner figure in the man is known as the 'anima' and that in the woman as the 'animus'. Both these figures appear in dreams in personified form, and if the man, for instance, fails to recognize the woman in himself, this may be projected upon an actual woman and he falls in love with her, or rather with his picture of her. It is by no means unusual for a woman to be irritated by the devoted attention of a man who insists on seeing in her the embodiment of his unfulfilled expectations.

Jung did not invent the concepts 'anima' and 'animus'. Novelists—for example, H. Rider Haggard (*She Who Must Be Obeyed*) and Thomas Hardy—were quite familiar with these ideas. Hardy published a tale on what today we might call the anima theme in 1892—when Jung was in his teens—and this has been reprinted.[30] As a portrait of the psychology of man and his anima it can be recommended.

One of the most significant studies of the opposites, and in particular the union of the opposites, is found in alchemy: 'The problem of opposites called up by the shadow plays a great—indeed, the decisive—rôle in alchemy, since it leads in the ultimate phase of the work to the union of opposites in the archetypal form of the *hieros gamos* or "chymical marriage". Here the supreme opposites, male and female (as in the Chinese Yang and Yin), are melted into a unity purified of all opposition'—a strange admixture—'and therefore uncorruptible'.[31]

29. *Aion* (1960), C. W., Vol. 9, Part II, p. 268.
30. Hardy, Thomas, *The Well-Beloved: A Sketch of a Temperament*, Macmillan (1952).
31. *Psychology and Alchemy* (1953), C. W., Vol. 12, pp. 36, 37.

In man the anima image, although experienced personally, is an archetypal phenomenon. Three main sources of this feminine quality in men and the masculine quality in women have been described: firstly, experience of individual women and men, and particularly of the mother or father; secondly, the inherited image of woman and of man; and thirdly, the latent principle of the opposite sex, physiological and psychological. Each sex carries the homologues of the other and each has a latent capacity to respond to the other, and to find completeness, fulfilment in the other.

These all too brief references to the opposites and their functioning should be supplemented by reading.[32] Yet they give an indication, a hint, of Jung's immense contribution to psychology, to psychopathology and to psychological treatment.

In an earlier chapter it was shown that co-operation between individuals possessing unrecognized differences in type can become impossible. Yet some rashly assume that they know all about psychology by the light of nature, and that plenty of common sense is the only reliable guide to personal and social adjustments. Women with abundant common sense, sound judgment, and goodwill may still find their day-by-day relations with colleagues difficult. Often in the background, unconscious and so projected, is the animus figure present in every woman. Experience shows that such a projection is likely to constellate the anima in the man, with disastrous results. A corresponding blindness in the man can also lead to disaster and recriminations in his attempted co-operation with the opposite sex. Good intentions must be supplemented by information, and Jung's research on the psychology of men and of women is an important chapter in his work.

In the course of analytical treatment, the paired opposites anima-animus emerge autonomously in dreams and in spontaneous paintings or drawings, and this should be taken as a sign that the activation of the unconscious has begun. These are not simple mat-

32. (a) *Two Essays on Analytical Psychology* (1953), C. W., Vol. 7, pp. 186 *et seq*; (b) *The Archetypes and the Collective Unconscious* (1959), C. W., Vol. 9, Part I, p. 54.

ters, understood in a moment. To reading must be added reflection and perception of the opposites as they appear in personal and collective experience.

Jung considers the individuation process as the most important goal in life; but the goal is not a fixed one, for the action continues throughout life. 'Life, being an energic process, needs the opposites, for without opposition there is, as we know, no energy.'[33] Individuation—its meaning and significance as a process of achievement—has been discussed earlier.[34] Its self-regulative movement is evident in the unceasing interplay of the opposites, essential to maintain balance; for the opposites are part of a movement and by no means isolated phenomena.

Consciousness brought face to face, confronted with the unconscious '. . . means open conflict and open collaboration at once. That, evidently, is the way human life should be. It is the old game of hammer and anvil: between them the patient iron is forged into an indestructible whole, an *individual*.'[35]

33. *Psychology and Religion: West and East* (1958), C. W., Vol. II, p. 197.
34. See pp. 84, 85 *et seq*.
35. *The Archetypes and the Collective Unconscious* (1959), C. W., Vol. 9 Part I, p. 288.

APPENDIX

Notable Occasions: An Account of Some of Jung's Birthdays, with the Transcription of a Broadcast Interview

I

ALL beginnings are important and so it is that birth and the anniversaries of the day of birth have, by custom, acquired a distinctive place in social life. In the later years birthdays provide an opportunity to do honour to those whose life and work are held in high esteem.

On two of Jung's birthdays colleagues and friends have composed and presented him with a birthday book, a *Festschrift*. Few have had the distinction of two such gifts.

The volume[1] given to Jung on his sixtieth birthday contained twenty-five essays and five plates. Some of the essays, such as the first by the late Toni Wolff, 'Introduction to the Main Principles of Complex Psychology', were books in themselves. A portrait-study of Jung by Barbara Hannah was chosen as the frontispiece. An unusual feature was a commentary, with two plates, on Jung's handwriting, by Gertrude Gilli.

Jung's house at Bollingen has many examples of his skill as a stone-carver, and one of these has a special significance in relation to his seventy-fifth birthday. On the terrace facing the lake is a stone seat, and at one end is placed a large square stone with three sides exposed. In June 1951 Jung told me the history of this stone. About the time of his seventy-fifth birthday he decided to enclose

1. *Die Kulturelle Bedeutung der Komplexen Psychologie* (1935), Verlag von Julius Springer.

part of the ground adjoining the house with a wall. For this purpose stones were brought by boat from the quarry on the opposite side of the lake. The stones had been carefully measured and the large square stone was to form part of the new wall. As the boat approached, Jung realized that the stone was not the correct shape for the wall; but to his delight he saw that it was a perfect cube. 'My heart leapt!' he exclaimed. 'That is the very thing I want!' It seemed almost miraculous. For Jung the quaternity, squareness, has immense significance: it is associated with completeness—for example, in the four functions or the four seasons. In alchemy the square represents symbolically the attainment of a higher unity.[2] In popular speech we have the familiar 'on the square' and 'stand four-square'.

Jung had the stone placed in its present position, and carved the three exposed surfaces. The carving on the front panel is in the form of a circle, a mandala—that is, 'the psychological expression of the totality of the self'.[3] In the center of the mandala is the *homunculus*, the strange 'dwarf motif', representing the unconscious formative powers.[4] In using this motif, Jung had in mind the power of the unconscious: 'Long experience has taught me not to know anything in advance and not to know better, but to let the unconscious take precedence.'[5] On the figure's right is the sun, and on the left the moon. Many other symbols appear, with the significant phrasing in Greek characters.

Of the two remaining panels, that on the right celebrates Jung's seventy-fifth birthday, and in Latin, deeply carved in the stone, he expresses gratitude for all life has given. Abbreviated medieval Latin is used on the remaining panel. Jung was quite at home in reading this difficult Latin script, which he originally learnt in order to read certain texts.

An eightieth birthday carries peculiar significance, and for Jung,

2. *Psychology and Alchemy* (1953), C. W., Vol. 12, pp. 119 *et seq.*
3. *The Archetypes and the Collective Unconscious* (1959), C. W., Vol. 9, Part I, p. 304.
4. *Psychology and Alchemy*, *op. cit.*, p. 180.
5. *The Archetypes and the Collective Unconscious*, *op. cit.*, Part I, p. 239.

as for his colleagues and friends, the celebration of this birthday was an occasion to be remembered.

Zürich was naturally the centre of interest, but there were gatherings in honour of Jung in many other places—London, New York, San Francisco, Calcutta and elsewhere.

Prior to the formal recognition of the birthday there was a private function confined to members of his family. There were only two absentees from this remarkable gathering of about forty relatives which included Professor and Mrs. Jung, their five children, seventeen of the nineteen grandchildren and two great-grandchildren. Two 'non-Jungs', staying at the time at Jung's house in Küsnacht-Zürich, were present—Miss Ruth Bailey, a family friend over many years, and myself ('You will have to be a member of the Jung family for the day,' remarked Jung to me on my arrival). It was at the formal recognition of the birthday that Jung was presented with the second birthday book. The two volumes of the *Festschrift*[6] had articles from thirty-two contributors. For some years the term 'complex psychology' was in current use, but there has been a change in terminology; the term 'analytical psychology' is now commonly used to indicate Jung's work, and this appears in the title of the volumes produced in his honour on this occasion.

Another presentation, from the C. G. Jung-Institute in Zürich, was an original papyrus, now known as the Jung Codex, and with it a volume containing photographic reproductions of each page of the papyrus, with a commentary. There are four books in this Codex, including the Gospel of Truth, by Valentinus himself. These are considered to be writings of the Gnostic School founded by Valentinus in the second century A.D. The manuscript has special importance for students of early Christian doctrine, particularly regarding the relations between Gnosticism, Judaism and Christianity. Jung's writings contain many references to Gnosticism and its relevance in the development of human thought.[7] The Jung codex is the latest of a group of thirteen volumes found at

6. *Studien zur Analytischen Psychologie C. G. Jungs* (1955), Rascher Verlag.
7. See p. 115.

Chenobskion in Upper Egypt. This papyrus had a chequered history, and for a time its whereabouts were uncertain. Eventually it was 're-discovered', and purchased so that it might be given to Jung. He was keenly interested in the Codex, and the gift was one he valued highly. Nevertheless, he felt the papyrus should be restored to the Egyptian Government and placed in the Coptic Museum in Cairo, so that the collection of thirteen volumes could be translated and made generally available. His fine gesture was much appreciated by the Egyptian Government, and the Codex has been returned to Egypt.

Those interested in the contents of these remarkable manuscripts, of which the Jung Codex is the latest, are referred to Jean Doresse's work.[8]

II

In the year 1894—he was then nineteen years of age—Jung acquired a first edition of a famous book by Erasmus (Adagiorum D. Erasmi, *Epitome*, 1563), and in it he came across the phrase *Vocatus atque non vocatus deus aderit* (Invoked or not invoked the god will be present). He was much attracted by the words and they may be seen cut in the stone lintel of his house in Küsnacht-Zürich and inscribed on his book-plate. Considerable speculation has been aroused by the phrase, and it has an interesting history. During the Peloponnesian Wars, the Lacedaemonians, before attacking Athens, consulted the Delphic Oracle, and the message they received, as translated by Erasmus from Greek into Latin, was: *Vocatus atque non vocatus deus aderit.* This saying became a proverb, and was applied when one wanted to hint at something that may happen in future whether desired or not, such as old age, death, etc.—in other words, an inevitable fate.

Jung had his first experience of a broadcast and television interview two days before his eightieth birthday. He had already declined an invitation from one broadcasting company, but, a little reluc-

8. Doresse, J., *The Secret Books of the Egyptian Gnostics*, Hollis and Carter (1960), pp. 137 *et seq.*, 238, 239.

tantly, he agreed to have a recorded talk with Mr. (Now Dr.) Stephen Black. The B.B.C. kindly handed over to me the copyright of the recording made in Jung's house, and so it is possible to print a verbatim account of the interview:

Black: Vocatus atque non vocatus deus aderit is a Latin translation of the Greek oracle, and, translated into English, it might read, 'Invoked or not invoked the god will be present', and in many ways this expresses the philosophy of Carl Jung. I am sitting now in a room in his house at Küsnacht, near Zürich, in Switzerland. And as I came in through the front door, I read this Latin translation of the Greek, carved in stone over the door. For this house was built by Professor Jung. How many years ago, Professor Jung?

Jung: Oh, almost fifty years ago.

Black: Why did you choose this to put over your front door?

Jung: Because I wanted to express the fact that I always feel unsafe, as if I'm in the presence of superior possibilities.

Black: Professor Jung is sitting opposite to me now. He is a large man, a tall man, and this summer reached his eightieth birthday. He has white hair, a very powerful face, with a small white moustache and deep brown eyes. He reminds me, with all respect, Professor Jung, of a typical peasant of Switzerland. What do you feel about that, Professor Jung?

Jung: Well, I think you are not just beside the mark. That is what I often have been called.

Black: And yet Professor Jung is a man whose reputation far transcends the frontiers of this little country. It's a reputation which isn't only European; it is world-wide and has made itself felt very considerably in the Far East. Professor Jung, how did you, as a doctor, become interested in psychological medicine?

Jung: Well, when I was a student of medicine I already then became interested in the psychological aspect—chiefly of mental diseases. I studied, beside my medical work, also philosophy—chiefly Kant, Schopenhauer and others. I found it very difficult in those days of scientific materialism to find a middle line between natural science or medicine and my philosophical interests. And in the last of my medical studies, just before my final exam, I discovered the short Introduction that Krafft-Ebing had written to his textbook of psychiatry, and suddenly I understood the connection between psychology or philosophy and medical science.

Black: This was due to Krafft-Ebing's Introduction to his textbook?

Jung: Yes; and it caused me tremendous emotion then. I was quite overwhelmed by a sudden sort of intuitive understanding. I wouldn't have been able to formulate it clearly then, but I felt I had touched a focus. And then on the spot I made up my mind to become a psychiatrist, because there was a chance to unite my philosophical interest with natural science and medical science; that was my chief interest from then on.

Black: Would you say that your sudden intuitive interest in something like that, your intuitive understanding, had to some extent been explained by your work during all the years since?

Jung: Oh, yes; absolutely, absolutely. But, as you know, such an intuitive moment contains the whole thing *in nucleo*. It is not clearly formulated; it's an indescribable totality; but this moment had been the real origin of my career as a medical psychological scientist.

Black: So it was in fact Krafft-Ebing and not Freud that started you off.

Jung: Oh yes, I became acquainted with Freud much later on.

Black: And when did you meet Freud?

Jung: That was only in 1907. I had some correspondence with him before that date, but I met him only in 1907 after I had written my book on *The Psychology of Dementia Praecox*.

Black: That was your first book?

Jung: That wasn't really my first book. The book on dementia praecox came after my doctor's thesis in 1904. And then my subsequent studies in the Association Experiment paved the way to Freud, because I saw that the behaviour of the complex provided the experimental basis for Freud's ideas on repression. And that was the reason and the possibility of our relationship.

Black: Would you like to describe to me that meeting?

Jung: Well, I went to Vienna and paid a visit to him, and our first meeting lasted thirteen hours.

Black: Thirteen hours?

Jung: For thirteen uninterrupted hours we talked and talked and talked. It was a *tour d'horizon*, in which I tried to make out Freud's peculiar mentality. He was a pretty strange phenomenon to me then, as he was to everybody in those days, and then I saw very clearly what his point of view was, and I also caught some glimpses already where I wouldn't join in.

Black: In what way was Freud a peculiar personality?

Jung: Well, that's difficult to say, you know. He was a very impressive man and obviously a genius. Yet you must know the peculiar atmosphere of Vienna in those days: it was the last days of the old Empire and Vienna was always spiritually and in every way a place of a very specific character. And particularly the Jewish intelligentsia was an impressive and peculiar phenomenon—particularly to us Swiss, you know. We were, of course, very different and it took me quite a while until I got it.

Black: Would you say, then, that the ideas and the philosophy which you have expressed have in their root something peculiarly Swiss?

Jung: Presumably. You know, our political neutrality has much to do with it. We were always surrounded by the great powers—those four powers, Germany, Austria, Italy and France—and we had to defend our independence, so the Swiss is characterized by that peculiar spirit of independence, and he always reserves his judgment. He doesn't easily imitate, and so he doesn't take things for granted.

Black: You are a man, Professor Jung, who reserves his judgment?

Jung: Always.

Black: In 1912 you wrote a book called *The Psychology of the Unconscious*, and it was at that time that you, as it were, dissociated yourself from Freud?

Jung: Well, that came about quite automatically because I developed certain ideas in that book which I knew Freud couldn't approve. Knowing his scientific materialism I knew that this was the sort of philosophy I couldn't subscribe to.

Black: Yours was the introvert, to use your own terminology?

Jung: No; mine was merely the empirical point of view. I didn't pretend to know anything, I wanted just to make the experience of the world to see what things are.

Black: Would you accuse Freud of having become involved in the mysticism of terms?

Jung: No; I wouldn't accuse him; it was just a style of the time. Thought, in a way, about psychological things was just, as it seems to me, impossible—too simple. In those days one talked of psychiatric illness as a sort of by-product of the brain. Joking with my pupils, I told them of an old text-book for the Medical Corps in the Swiss Army which gave a description of the brain, saying it looked like a dish of macaroni, and the steam from the macaroni was the psyche. That is the old view, and it is far too simple. So I said: 'Psychology is the science of the psychic phenomena.' We can't observe whether these phenomena are produced by the brain, or whether they are there in their own right—they are just what they are. I have no theory about the origin of the psyche. I take phenomena as they are and I try to describe them and to classify them, and my terminology is an empirical terminology, like the terminology in botany or zoology.

Black: You've travelled a great deal?

Jung: Yes; a lot. I have been with Navajo Indians in North America, and in North Africa, in East and Central Africa, the Sudan and Egypt, and in India.

Black: Do you feel that the thought of the East is in any way more advanced than the thought in the West?

Jung: Well, you see, the thought of the East cannot be compared with the thought in the West; it is incommensurable. It is something else.

Black: In what way does it differ, then?

Jung: Well, they are far more influenced by the basic facts about psychology than we are.

Black: That sounds more like your philosophy.

Jung: Oh, yes; quite. That is my particular understanding of the East, and the East can appreciate my ideas better, because they are better prepared to see the truth of the psyche. Some think there is nothing in the mind when the child is born, but I say everything is in the mind when the child is born, only it isn't conscious yet. It is there as a potentiality. Now, the East is chiefly based upon that potentiality.

Black: Does this contribute to the happiness of people one way or the other? Are people happier in themselves in the East?

Jung: I don't think that they are happier than we are. You see, they have no end of problems, of diseases and conflicts; that is the human lot.

Black: Is their unhappiness based upon their psychological difficulties, like ours, or is it more based upon their physical environment, their economics?

Jung: Well, you see, there is no difference between, say, unfavourable social conditions and unfavourable psychological conditions. We may be, in the West, in very favourable social conditions, and we are as miserable as possible—inside. We have the trouble from the inside. They have it perhaps more from the outside.

Black: And have you any views on the reason for this misery we suffer here?

Jung: Oh, yes; there are plenty of reasons. Wrong values—we believe in things which are not really worthwhile. For instance, when a man has only one automobile and his neighbour has two, then that is a very sad fact and he is apt to get neurotic about it.

Black: In what other ways are our values at fault?

Jung: Well, all ambitions and all sorts of things—illusions, you know, of any description. It is impossible to name all those things.

Black: What is your view, Professor Jung, on the place of women in society in the Western world?

Jung: In what way? The question is a bit vague.

Black: You said just now, Professor Jung, that some of our difficulties arose out of wrong values, and I'm trying to find out whether you feel those wrong values arise in men as a result of the demands of women.

Jung: Sometimes, of course, they do, but very often it is the female in a man that is misleading him. The anima in man, his feminine side, of which he is truly unaware, is causing his moods, his resentments, his prejudices.

Black: So that the woman who wants two cars because a neighbour has two cars, is only stimulating . . . ?

Jung: No, perhaps she simply voices what he has felt for a long time. He wouldn't dare to express it, but she voices it—she is, perhaps, naive enough to say so.

Black: And what does the man express of the woman's animus?

Jung: Well, he is definitely against it, because the animus always gets his 'goat', it calls forth his anima affects and anima moods; they get on each other's nerves. Listen to a conversation between a man and wife when there is a certain amount of emotion about them. You hear all the wonderful arguments of an anima in the man; he talks then like a woman, and she talks like a man, with very definite opinions and knows all about it.

Black: Do you feel that there's any hope of adjusting this between a man and a woman, if they understand it in your terms?

Jung: Well, you see, that is one of the main reasons why I have developed a certain psychology of relationship—for instance the relationship in marriage, and how a man and his wife should understand each other or how they misunderstand each other practically. That's a whole chapter of psychology and not an unimportant one.

Black: Which is the basic behaviour? The Eastern?

Jung: Neither. The East is just as one-sided in its way as the West is in its way. I wouldn't say that the position of the woman in the East is more natural or better than with us. Civilizations have developed styles. For instance, a Frenchman or an Italian or an Englishman show very different and very characteristic ways in dealing with their respective wives. I suppose you have seen English marriages, and you know how an English gentleman would deal with his wife in the event of trouble, for instance; and if you compare this with an Italian, you will see all the difference in the world. You know, Italy cultivates its emotions. Italians like emotions and they dramatize their emotions. Not so the English.

Black: And in India or Malaya?

Jung: In India, presumably the same, I had no chance to assist in a domestic problem in India, happily enough. It was a holiday from Europe, where I had had almost too much to do with domestic problems of my patients—that sort of thing was my daily bread.

Black: Would you say, then, as a scientific observation that there is, in fact, less domestic trouble in the East than in the West?

Jung: I couldn't say that. There is another kind of domestic problem, you know. They live in crowds together in one house, twenty-five people in one little house, and the grandmother on top of the show, which is a terrific problem. Happily enough, we have no such things over here.

Black: At the end of his life, Freud, one feels, had some dissatisfaction with the nature of psychoanalysis, the length of time involved in the treatment of mental illness and so on. Have you, now you're eighty years old, felt any dissatisfaction with your work?

Jung: No; I couldn't say so. I know I'm not dissatisfied at all, but I have no illusions about the difficulty of human nature. You see, Freud was always a bit impatient; he always hoped to find some short-cut. And I knew that is just the thing we would not find, because anything that is good is expensive. It takes time, it requires your patience and no end of it. I can't say I am dissatisfied. And so I always thought anything, if it is something good, will take time, will demand all your patience, it will be expensive. You can't get around it.

Black: How did you meet your wife? Is she connected with your work?

Jung: Well, I met her when she was quite a young girl, about fifteen or sixteen, and I just happened to see her, and I said to a friend of mine—I was twenty-one then—I said, 'That girl is my wife.'

Black: Before you'd spoken to her?

Jung: Yes. 'That's my wife'. I knew it. I saw her on top of a staircase and I knew: 'That is my wife.'

Black: How many children have you got?

Jung: Five children, nineteen grandchildren, and two great-grandchildren.

Black: Has any of this large family followed in your footsteps?

Jung: Well, my son is an architect and an uncle of mine was an architect. None has studied medicine—all my daughters married—but they are very interested and they 'got it' at home, you see, through the atmosphere. One nephew is a medical doctor.

Black: Were you interested in architecture at all?

Jung: Oh, yes; very much so. I have built with my own hands; I learned the work of a mason. I went to a quarry to learn how to split stones—big rocks.

Black: And actually laying bricks, laying the stones?

Jung: Oh, well, in Europe we work with stone. I did actually lay stones and built part of my house up in Bollingen.

Black: Why did you do that?

Jung: I wanted to handle and get the feeling of the stone and to touch the earth—I worked a lot in the garden, I have chopped wood, felled trees and all that. I liked sailing and rowing and mountain climbing when I was young.

Black: Could you explain what you think the origins of this desire to touch the earth? We in England have it very much; every Englishman has his little garden. We all love the earth.

Jung: Of course. Well, you know, that is—how can we explain it?—you love the earth and the earth loves you. And therefore the earth brings forth. That is so even with the peasant who wants to make his field fertile, and in the night of the full moon he sleeps with his wife in the furrow.

Black: Professor Jung, what do you think will be the effect upon the world of living, as we have been living, and may still have to live, under the threat of the hydrogen bomb?

Jung: Well, that's a very great problem. I think the West is more affected by it than the East, because the East has a very different attitude to death and destruction. Think, for instance, of the fact that practically the whole of India believes in reincarnation, so when you lose this life you have plenty of others. It doesn't matter so much. Moreover, this world is illusion anyhow, and if you can get rid of it, it isn't so bad. And if you hope for a further life, well, you have untold possibilities ahead of you. Since in the West there is one life only, therefore I can imagine that the West is more disturbed by the possibility of utter destruction than the East. We have to lose only one life and we are by no means assured of a number of other lives to follow. The greater part of the European population doesn't even believe in immortality any more and so, once destroyed, forever destroyed. That explains a great deal of the reaction in the West. We are more vulnerable by our lack of knowledge and contact with the deepest strata of the psyche; but the East is better defended in that way, because it is based upon the fundamental facts of the human soul and believes more in it and in its possibilities than the West. And that is a point of uncertainty in the West. It is a very critical point.

III

Jung's eighty-fifth birthday in July 1960 was marked by several social functions, and these were spread over some weeks in order to minimize fatigue for the chief participant. On the actual birthday Jung entertained his children, grandchildren and great-grandchildren—now numbering ten–at the family house. A rare honour was conferred on Jung the following day. A banquet was given for him by the local authority of Küsnacht-Zürich (the equivalent of the Town Council) and he was elected *Ehrenburgher*, which corresponds to being made a Freeman of the township. During the last one hundred and fifty years only two others have had this distinction, and they were natives of Küsnacht. As a rule, only one who is born locally can become *Ehrenburgher*. But an exception was made for Jung, who, although of Swiss nationality, had been born in another canton. The significance of this honour may escape foreigners; but it is evidence—if such were needed—of the attitude towards their distinguished fellow-townsman of those who have been his neighbours for more than sixty years.

Acknowledgments

For permission to make use of material, the author is grateful to:

Miss Ruth Bailey for the photograph of Professor Jung which is reproduced as the cover image.

Professor A. C. Mace for extracts from his address at a celebration in honour of Professor Jung's eightieth birthday.

Dr. Stephen Black and the British Broadcasting Corporation for the transcription of an interview with Professor Jung.

The author also expresses thanks to the publishers and authors listed in the bibliography for extracts and quotations from their works.

Abbreviation:
C. W. indicates the *Collected Works* of C. G. Jung

Bibliography

George Allen and Unwin:

Freud, S., *Introductory Lectures of Psychoanalysis* (1923).

Glover, E., *Freud or Jung* (1950).

Lévy-Bruhl, L., *The 'Soul' of the Primitive* (1928).

Russell, Bertrand, *History of Western Philosophy* (1946).

Wittles, F., *Sigmund Freud* (1934).

Ballière, Tindall, and Cox:

Jung, C. G., *Collected Papers on Analytical Psychology* (1920).

Benn:

Jones, E., *Psycho-Analysis* (1929).

The Editor of *Brain*:

Jung, C. G., and Peterson, W. F., 'Psycho-physical Investigations with the Galvanometer and Pneumograph in Normal and Insane Individuals', (1907) XXX, pp. 118, 153–218.

The Editor of the *British Medical Journal*:

Bennet, E. A., 'Archetype and *Aion*, (review) (1960), I, p. I, 484.

Cambridge University Press:

Hart, Bernard, *Psychopathology* (1929).

Cassell:

Mayer-Gross, W., Slater, Eliot, Roth, Martin, *Clinical Psychiatry* (1951).

Character and Personality:

Jung, C. G., 'Sigmund Freud in His Historical Setting', I (1932).

James Clarke:

Matthews, W. R. (and others), *William Temple: An Estimate and an Appreciation* (1946).

Clarendon Press:

Leibniz, G. W., *The Monadology and Other Philosophical Writings* (1898).

Collins:

Teilhard de Chardin, Pierre, *Le Milieu Divin* (1960).

Dover Publications:

Cumont, Franz, *The Mysteries of Mithra* (1956).

Hogarth Press:

Freud, S., *Civilization and Its Discontents* (1930). *An Autobiographical Study* (1935). *Moses and Monotheism* (1939). *An Outline of Psycho-Analysis* (1949).

Sharpe, Ella, Dream Analysis (1937).
Jones, E., *A Symposium: Psychotherapeutics* (1910). *Sigmund Freud*, Vol. I (1953). *Sigmund Freud*, Vol. II (1955). *Sigmund Freud*, Vol. III (1957). *Free Associations* (1959). *Essays in Applied Psychoanalysis* (1953).
Hollis and Carter:
Doresse, Jean, *The Secret Books of the Egyptian Gnostics* (1960).
Horizon:
Glover, E., XI, No. 63 (1943).
The Editor of the *Journal of Analytical Psychology*:
Bennet, E. A., 'Jung's Concept of the Time Stream' (1960).
Lewis, Sir Aubrey, 'Jung's Early Work' (1957).
Kegan Paul:
Jung, C. G., *Essays on Contemporary Events* (1947).
Kegan Paul, Trench, Trübner:
The Secret of the Golden Flower, translated and explained by Richard Wilhelm, with a European Commentary by C. G. Jung (1931).
Jung, C. G., *Contributions to Analytical Psychology* (1928). *Psychological Types* (1933). *Modern Man in Search of a Soul* (1933). *The Integration of the Personality* (1940).
The Editor of the *Lancet*:
Comfort, A., 'Darwin and Freud' (1960), II, p. 107.
Longmans Green & Co.:
Dalbiez, R., *Psychoanalytical Method and the Doctrine of Freud* (1945).
James, William, *The Varieties of Religious Experience* (1904).
Mace, Professor A. C.
Macmillan:
Hardy, Thomas, *The Well-Beloved: A Sketch of a Temperament* (1952).
Nervous and Mental Disease Publishing Co.:
Jung, C. G., *Psychology of Dementia Praecox* (1936).
New York Times:
Sykes, Gerald, book review (2nd August 1953).
Pelican Books:
Fordham, F., *An Introduction to Jung's Psychology* (1953).
The Editor of the *Psychiatric Quarterly:*
Harms, Ernest, 'Carl Gustav Jung—Defender of Freud and the Jews' (1946), 20, p. 199.
Barrie and Rockliff:
Philp, H. L., *Freud and Religious Belief* (1956). *Jung and the Problem of Evil* (1958).
Ronald Press:
Alexander, F., and French, T. M., *Psychoanalytic Therapy* (1946).
Routledge and Kegan Paul:
Jung, C. G., *The Collected Works:*
Vol. I, *Psychiatric Studies* (1957).
Vol. 3, *The Psychogenesis of Mental Disease* (1960).

Vol. 5, *Symbols of Transformation* (1956).
Vol. 7, *Two Essays on Analytical Psychology* (1953).
Vol. 8, *The Structure and Dynamics of the Psyche* (1960).
Vol. 9, Part I: *The Archetypes and the Collective Unconscious* (1959). Part II: *Aion: Researches into the Phenomenology of the Self* (1959).
Vol. 11, *Psychology and Religion: West and East* (1958).
Vol. 12, *Psychology and Alchemy* (1953).
Vol. 16, *The Practice of Psychotherapy* (1954).
Vol. 17, *The Development of Personality* (1954).
Jung, C. G., *The Undiscovered Self* (1958). *Flying Saucers: A Modern Myth of Things Seen in the Skies* (1959).
The I Ching or Book of Changes, translated by Richard Wilhelm, rendered into English by Cary F. Baynes, Foreword by C. G. Jung (1951).
Jacobi, Jolande, *Complex/Archetype/Symbol in the Psychology of C. G. Jung* (1959).
Progoff, Ira, *Jung's Psychology and Its Social Meaning* (1953).
St. Bartholomew's Hospital Journal:
Jung, C. G., 'The Concept of the Collective Unconscious', 44 (1936).
Springer, Julius:
Die Kulturelle Bedeutung der Komplexen Psychologie (1935).

Index

Printed in Great Britain
by Amazon

83645386R00113